FISHING
AND
FISHERMEN

A Guide for Family Historians

M a r t i n   W i l c o x

Pen & Sword
FAMILY HISTORY

First published in Great Britain in 2009 by
PEN & SWORD FAMILY HISTORY
an imprint of
Pen & Sword Books Ltd
47 Church Street
Barnsley
South Yorkshire
S70 2AS

ISBN 978 1 84415 988 8

A CIP catalogue record for this book is
available from the British Library.

Typeset in Palatino and Optima by
Phoenix Typesetting, Auldgirth, Dumfriesshire

Printed and bound in England by
CPI UK

Pen & Sword Books Ltd incorporates the Imprints of
Pen & Sword Aviation, Pen & Sword Maritime, Pen & Sword Military,
Wharncliffe Local History, Pen & Sword Select, Pen & Sword Military Classics
and Leo Cooper.

For a complete list of Pen & Sword titles please contact
PEN & SWORD BOOKS LIMITED
47 Church Street, Barnsley, South Yorkshire, S70 2AS, England
E-mail: enquiries@pen-and-sword.co.uk
Website: www.pen-and-sword.co.uk

This book should be returned to any branch of the
Lancashire County Library on or before the date shown

ZBS. LOCAL

Lancashire County Library
Bowran Street
Preston PR1 2UX

FAMILY HISTORY FROM PEN & SWORD

Tracing Your Yorkshire Ancestors
Rachel Bellerby

Tracing Your Royal Marine Ancestors
Richard Brooks and Matthew Little

Tracing Your Army Ancestors
Simon Fowler

A Guide to Military History on the Internet
Simon Fowler

Tracing Your Northern Ancestors
Keith Gregson

Your Irish Ancestors
Ian Maxwell

Tracing Your Air Force Ancestors
Phil Tomaselli

Tracing Your Jewish Ancestors
Rosemary Wenzerul

CONTENTS

ACKNOWLEDGEMENTS

I should like to thank Rupert Harding and his colleagues at Pen and Sword for their assistance and support, and Simon Fowler for his invaluable advice. Thanks are also due to Elizabeth Stone, who edited the text.

My interest in fishing history began during my time as a post-graduate student in the Maritime Historical Studies Centre of the University of Hull, and from there I should like to thank Drs David J. Starkey, Robb Robinson and Richard Gorski for their assistance, as well as John Nicholls and Michaela Barnard. I am especially grateful for permission to use images from the collection of the late Dr Basil Greenhill.

I must also acknowledge support from my colleagues at Greenwich Maritime Institute, who have allowed me the time to research this book and provided much appreciated advice, especially Professors Sarah Palmer and Roger Knight, and Glyn Williams, Suzanne Bowles and James Davey.

Numerous institutions have been most helpful, and I should particularly like to thank staff at the National Archives, North-East Lincolnshire Archives and Brixham Heritage Museum, and also Jerry Michell of the National Maritime Museum. Hugh Murphy, editor of the *Mariner's Mirror*, kindly gave permission for me to reproduce images.

Finally, I should like to acknowledge the practical assistance given by Jeff Sutton and Martin Jury, and the moral support of many other friends by whom it has been a pleasure to be distracted from the writing.

Responsibility for any errors and omissions is, of course, my own.

PREFACE

Fishing exerts an enduring fascination for many people. At various times in its history, it has been highly significant in economic, cultural and even political terms, and it remains so to this day.

Part of the appeal of fishing, perhaps, is that it is an unusual business. It is not purely an extractive industry, like mining, although at times it has been treated as such. Nor is it a manufacturing industry, or a service industry like transport. Instead, it contains elements of all three. Fishing is to an extent unique.

But there are less analytical reasons. Fishermen are the last group in the developed world whose livelihood depends on hunting wild creatures, pitting their skills against the often hostile marine environment. Nowadays, with the use of sophisticated fish-finding equipment and nets many times the size fishermen only a few decades ago could deploy, the struggle can seem a rather unequal one, but even so, the success of any fishing venture is never guaranteed and the penalties for failure are very often high. Fishing is a deeply risky business, both in economic and in personal terms. Many men take on large debts to buy their vessels, and a poor season's fishing can easily ruin them. Down the centuries, that has not changed. Nor have the physical risks, for even now, with modern safety equipment and vessels far better able to cope with stormy weather and dangerous waters than any before, fishing is the most dangerous peacetime occupation. In the 1880s, it was calculated that four in every thousand fishermen in the United Kingdom were lost each year, a death rate said to be ten times that of mining. In the early twenty-first century, it has been calculated that 103 in every 100,000 fishermen will die at work, a quarter of the death rate in late Victorian times, but still almost double that of the second most dangerous occupation, merchant seafaring, and fifty times that of the average shore job.

Not only is fishing dangerous but it is also a highly skilled

One of the last of the classic sailing trawlers, Brixham *smack* Encourage, *built in 1926. (Basil Greenhill Collection, Maritime Historical Studies Centre, University of Hull)*

occupation, no less so now than at any time in its history. A successful skipper needs a detailed knowledge of fishing grounds, target species, the law of the sea and the regulations governing fishing, the markets he is likely to sell in, his crew, his vessel and its complex and expensive gear. All this knowledge needs to be gained, retained and deployed when necessary, in a highly pressured and occasionally critically dangerous environment. That is no less true of the modern skipper in the wheelhouse of a million-pound boat than it was of the Victorian skipper, at the tiller of a wooden sailing vessel, or an Elizabethan fisherman setting out on a long and hazardous Atlantic crossing to the cod fisheries of Newfoundland.

With the danger and the skill comes a degree of romance, partly perhaps because of the appeal of an individual pitting his strength and expertise against the elements, but also because of the picturesque qualities of fishing. Today, working fishing ports often have viewing galleries from where you can watch the vessels loading supplies, unloading fish, being repaired. Even modern fishing craft generate interest. More picturesque still are those images from the past: the sight of fleets of luggers leaving small coves in the southwest for the grounds, or of sailing trawlers and drifters in the North Sea pressing on hard for home, heeling over in the breeze with spray flying from the bows. The popularity of postcards and pictures of fishing vessels from times gone by bears witness to their enduring appeal.

Fishing has never been among the largest industries in Britain, in terms of the numbers employed or the capital invested, and although the herring trade was a staple of the medieval European economy, fishing ranked well behind agriculture in Britain. Fishing has, however, been immensely significant for much of the coast of Britain. Most coastal villages have at one time or another been home and operating base to a few fishermen; some settlements, indeed, were established precisely for this purpose. Fishing was, and is, vital to the economy of many parts of the coast, and several towns, most famously Grimsby, owe much of their development to the expansion and transformation of the industry in the nineteenth and twentieth centuries.

About this book

This short work has two main purposes. In the first place, it seeks to give a short outline history of the industry, as an introduction for those not familiar with it and, also, as a source of reference. Secondly, and more importantly, this is a guide for those seeking to research fishing and fishermen, and especially those who want to trace ancestors who worked within the industry. To this end, each chapter introduces one or more bodies of primary source material, and for each gives a short explanation of its provenance, a guide to the uses that can be made of it by researchers and some practical tips on how to access the records and what you may find within them. Inevitably, the scope of this work represents its author's main interests and areas of expertise. The emphasis is on the modern period, as it is really only since the nineteenth century that large bodies of documents were systematically generated that will be of use to the family historian. Whaling is not covered in this volume, for this has virtually always been a separate industry from sea fishing, and it has its own distinctive body of literature and sources that can be used in research. River and estuarial fisheries are covered here, but perhaps in less detail than their historical importance deserves. The period of their greatest significance was one before a great deal of documentation was needed or created, which makes them more difficult to research. The fisheries of Ireland, too, receive less coverage than they deserve, for which I can plead no excuse beyond the limitations of my own knowledge.

Some problems and definitions

Fishing is a complex and diverse subject. Even in quite limited geographical areas, fisheries have varied greatly, and some of this diversity is still evident now. It is important to understand at least some of the reasons for this, because they have shaped both the industry and the ways in which you go about researching it.

The British Isles sit on the edge of the North West European Continental Shelf, one of the largest areas of shallow seas on the planet. Thanks to a favourable combination of climate, currents and run-off of nutrients from the surrounding lands, the waters around these islands are some of the most productive fishing grounds on earth. Over time, they have yielded vast catches of a wide variety of species, but not all of these can be found in all places or at all times. Many demersal fish – those which live on or near the seabed – are found all around the coast. Cod, for instance, has been caught from most British fishing ports at one time or another. Ling, however, is found only further north, meaning that although Scottish fishermen have frequently pursued it, English fishermen have done so far less often. The opposite is true of hake, which is found principally off the south-west and was a staple of the Cornish fishing industry. Pelagic fish are shoaling species that dwell nearer the sea's surface, and migrate with the seasons. Again, there are regional differences in where they can be found. Herring is found all around the British Isles, but pilchards only off the south-west, and mackerel is also primarily a preserve of the south. Shellfish, too, depend on favourable breeding grounds, which govern where they can be caught, hence the extensive oyster beds around the Thames estuary and the large-scale fishery for cockles in the north-west. Different fish are caught with different types of gear, which in turn require varying forms of boat. A drifter, used in the past for catching pelagic fish, might look superficially similar to a trawler of the same age, but was in fact very different.

If the species available for catching in any given locality help to determine the character of its fisheries, the same is true of the other end of the process: the opportunities to market the catch. Until the nineteenth century, these opportunities were relatively limited. Fish is a highly perishable commodity, and before the development of the railways the cost and slowness of contemporary transport limited the sale of fresh fish largely to areas within a few miles of the coast. Large coastal towns have often stimulated the fishing effort nearby, the classic example being the rise of trawling in the south-east and the Thames estuary, which was made worthwhile by the almost limitless London market nearby, but only after the mid-nineteenth century was the need to land fish near the market removed. Before this, anything not for immediate consumption had to be cured, usually by salting, drying or smoking. Cured fish, in fact, has rarely been a major item of consumption in Britain, and its importance to the fisheries has been based on exports, whose markets also shape the industry. By and large, the east coast of Britain is more populous than the west, the terrain is easier to transport goods over and historically it has been better integrated into the main European trade routes. These factors account for the earlier development of commercial fishing in the east than the west.

Other factors, too, help to shape the fishing industry in different places. 'He who would go to sea for pleasure,' wrote Dr Johnson, 'would go to hell for a pastime.' Seafaring has not infrequently been

Oyster-dredger Mayflower, *photographed in 1952. Small boats fished inshore under sail well into the twentieth century, and a few do to the present day. (Basil Greenhill Collection)*

a product of lack of opportunities to do much else, and fishing is no exception. Many fishing settlements were, and sometimes are, isolated places where few other opportunities for employment existed. Social exclusion has also sometimes driven men into the fisheries. Much of the Victorian trawling fleet was manned by young men whose choices were limited to the workhouse or the fishing port.

Where fishing shared facilities with other activities, this too shaped its character. Dover experienced difficulties as a fishing port, for instance, because its harbour had to be shared with the cross-channel packets, and the two activities came into conflict. At around the same time, there was conflict in Scarborough between the needs of the fishing industry and the town's desire to attract wealthy tourists, who might have been put off by cartloads of fish being hauled through the town to the railway station. At Plymouth, practice shelling from the naval battery sank at least one fishing vessel, and several others had near misses with warships out conducting high-speed trials. More prosaically, the facilities available to fishermen influence their activities. Where there is no harbour boats must be worked from the beach, and they must be built for that purpose, which limits their size and uses. A viable inshore fishery can be conducted from the beach; distant-water fishing cannot.

Much of this matters less now than it did in the past. The railways and then the rise of the lorry and the private car have lessened the isolation of most places and, with the ability to travel and market the product at a greater distance, local market conditions shape fishing less than they once did. Indeed, in the last few decades the fish trades have gone global, with valuable fish being moved around the world by air freight and boats arranging landings in the most lucrative places by radio, whilst still at sea. Fishing technology has come on in leaps and bounds and with it some of the unique regional types of boat have fallen out of use, although by no means all. Some distinctive local customs and traditions have also died out, but again, certainly not all, and fishing retains much of its idiosyncratic variety.

Fisheries have been classified in various ways over the years – by species, type of gear and location. You will come across such terms as 'inshore fishing', and 'middle-water trawling', reflecting a classification by area, which is problematic because until comparatively recently most fishing was conducted within a few miles of land and might be termed 'inshore', whilst although there has been talk of 'deep sea' fishing for a long time, it is only recently that truly deep waters have been fished. Classifications such as these mainly reflect the priorities of the fishing industry in the nineteenth and twentieth centuries. This book classifies fishing under four main headings. First, 'inshore' fisheries refer to fishing in rivers and estuaries and in coastal waters, generally involving hours rather than days at sea. 'Offshore' fisheries are those conducted in waters around the British Isles but at a greater distance from shore and for longer periods of time. Most British sea fisheries of the nineteenth century would fall into this category, such as the developing trawl fishery in the North Sea. 'Distant-water' fishing is that conducted at a long distance from home, on the continental shore of another country or continent, such as the sixteenth- and seventeenth-century fisheries on the Grand Banks of Newfoundland, or the distant-water sector of the twentieth-century trawl fishery. 'Deep-sea' fishing refers to fishing off the continental shelf, something which has only become feasible in the last half-century.

Occasional confusion over definitions reflects another facet of the study of fishing, namely the lack of academic attention paid to it. Until recently, historians of British maritime history have rather tended to overlook many of the more mundane activities, fishing included. Photogenic though they may be, fishing vessels lack the glamour of ocean liners and battle fleets, and as a result they have often been ignored. It is possible to read several books on Britain's maritime past and come away none the wiser about the fact that a century ago Britain had the largest and most successful fishing industry in the world, employing some 35,000 men at sea and tens of thousands more in related activities ashore. Only in the last twenty years or so has interest in the subject picked up, and with it the amount of published research. Detailed local studies using previously unused records have filled in some gaps in our knowledge, especially of medieval fishing, and the larger archives relating to more recent fisheries have been mined for information to inform national studies of important areas of the industry, but much still remains to be done. In particular, a comprehensive and readable short history of the industry still needs to be written.

There are, then, fewer well-trodden pathways for the researcher of fishing and fishermen to follow than there are for many other industries, and there are areas in which much still remains to be discovered, or can only be speculated on. Evidence relating to fishing before modern times is fragmentary, and for some areas of activity it is nigh-on non-existent, because until recently there was little need for records to be kept. From an early date, some merchants kept written records of their dealings, local authorities of various sorts maintained some records, usually of legal disputes, taxes paid and so on, but little was recorded relating to the fishing itself, least of all by fishermen themselves, many of whom were illiterate. Even in more recent times, with a more literate society increasingly reliant on the written record, most records relate to the largest and most important activities such as the nascent trawl fisheries of the nineteenth century. These were the activities which required intervention and regulation by government. Fishing for subsistence alone, or inshore fisheries conducted from remote areas and producing only a small surplus for the market largely escaped the attentions of legislators, the regulations made by whom are usually the reason for the generation of the documents we now use to research fishing. The records relating to fishing, then, are uneven in what they cover. They are made more so by varying rates of survival, which are in some measure a matter of chance. Some bodies of records have been preserved intact in public archives, others are still in private hands, and others still have been disposed of in clear-outs of company and family documents or otherwise destroyed.

The surviving records are widely dispersed across the country. There has never been one central body administering fishing, and therefore there is no one large archive from which most information can be obtained, unlike with, say, the armed forces or even merchant shipping. At various times, government departments in England and Scotland have set out to regulate the industry on a regional or even national scale, and their papers form a very important part of the material available to the researcher, but much material has also been generated by private businesses whose records are distributed around an array of repositories.

Researching fishing and fishermen, then, can be challenging, and it can involve a fair amount of detective work. Nevertheless, ample material exists to make the fishing industry a fruitful field of study, and much has not been researched in great detail yet, which gives the added interest of potentially discovering something new. My hope in writing this book is that those who do have an interest in fishing or an ancestor who worked within the industry will find it a useful introduction to an underrated subject, and a helpful starting point for their own research.

Chapter One

GETTING STARTED

1.1 First steps

The best way to start any piece of research is to take stock of what you already know, and what you can find out from family members and papers you or they might have in their possession.

Find out and write down the full names of any ancestors in the fishing industry that you know of, along with any nicknames, changes of name and so on. Ideally, you should also try to find out the dates and places of their birth, marriage and death. Then try to discover as much as possible about their careers. In particular, you should be looking for the port that they worked from, the names of any ships they might have worked aboard, details of any incidents they are said to have been involved in and any other details that might come to hand even if at first these seem insignificant. For instance, even a chance reference to a species of fish can tell you roughly what branch of the industry your ancestor was engaged in, which in turn gives you a better idea of what records you might come to consult.

1.2 Background research

It is always easier to appreciate the importance of details you find of someone's career if you know a little about the industry, so read up on fishing, and in particular the part of the industry that your

ancestor worked in. This book will give you a very general introduction, and at the end of each chapter I give references to other
books that will give you much more detail. Inevitably with a less
popular subject such as fishing, some of these are quite rare,
although I have tried to avoid recommending very obscure titles.
Websites such as Book Finder (www.bookfinder.com) and
AbeBooks (www.abebooks.com) are useful in tracking down copies
of older and less common works.

Books, especially more academic tomes, can be expensive.
Thankfully, you should be able to obtain most of what you need
through public libraries. For rarer works you may have to use an
academic library. Most university libraries offer associate member-
ships, albeit usually for a fee, whilst the British Library (www.bl.uk)
holds copies of virtually every book published in English.

In addition to reading up on the subject, there are many excellent

*Brixham
Heritage
Museum, one of
many local
museums
featuring
displays on the
local fishing
industry,
including
documents, ship
models and
various
artefacts.
(Brixham
Heritage
Museum)*

general guides to family history research which will help you to structure and organize your research and give you a better idea of how to use generic sources such as parish records and the census, which for reasons of space cannot be discussed here. Many of those sources have books devoted to them, whose titles are mentioned in the text.

There are, of course, many museums large and small around the country that feature fishing to varying degrees. The largest museum specifically dedicated to fishing is the National Fishing Heritage Centre in Grimsby, whose displays mainly relate to the trawl fisheries of the nineteenth and twentieth centuries, and which is well worth a visit. North of the border, there is the Scottish Fisheries Museum at Anstruther. Many local museums, maritime museums and general local heritage museums alike, have displays on local fisheries and are always worth a visit. As well as their own collections, many are good places to obtain local history books, and often have links with or are staffed by local historians who are frequently very knowledgeable, invariably happy to share their expertise with an interested researcher and may well be able to point you in the direction of useful and obscure sources of information. In all cases, local museums are invaluable repositories of information, and most deserve to be far better supported than they are.

1.3 The Internet

The Internet is becoming an increasingly valuable tool for historical and genealogical research. Here I have assumed that readers have Internet access at home, but, if this is not the case, public libraries have public computers, and often training sessions on how to get the best out of the Internet. This is not difficult, but there is a knack to finding the information you want and you need to treat information critically because although there is a lot of very helpful material out there, there is also much that is dubious, or just plain wrong. Peter Christian's book *The Genealogist's Internet* (National Archives, 2005) is a useful guide to getting the best out of this source of information.

The main use for the Internet is seeking out collections of documents, as well as museums and other places that will help you research fishing in general, if not find an individual. Most museums and archives maintain websites with at least a summary of their collections, and an increasing number of archives' catalogues can now be found online. You will find the addresses of useful websites distributed throughout the text, but those given here are not exhaustive, so do use search engines such as google (www. google.com) to seek out more. In particular, searching on types of documents you intend to use is often worthwhile, since there are many online source guides.

Most government departments and other official organizations with responsibility for overseeing fishing maintain websites, which often contain useful information. Some also maintain online archives of past reports and other material, in a few cases dating back many years. Examples include the Sea Fish Industry Authority (www.seafish.org), and the Marine and Fisheries Authority (www.mfa.gov.uk), which maintains lists of fishing vessels since the 1990s, and sea fisheries statistics and a few reports dating back to the nineteenth century. The Fisheries Research Service (www.marlab.ac.uk) is a mine of information on all aspects of the Scottish fisheries. For researching the fishing industry in the recent past, sites such as these are an essential resource.

Information relating to fisheries in the past is much less comprehensive, although useful information can be found, mainly relating to the nineteenth and twentieth centuries. There is, for example, a very good essay on the nineteenth-century Scottish fisheries on the fisheries section of www.historyshelf.org, and many local history sites contain pages on fishing in the area, although the quality of these does vary.

Unlike some subjects, fisheries history has few sites devoted to it and you will not find many discussions of it on the main genealogy forums. Nevertheless, it is worth looking at sites such as Genuki (www.genuki.org.uk/) and Rootsweb (www.rootsweb.ancestry. com/), as well as local genealogy sites for areas where your ancestors lived and worked.

Another good idea is simply to put an ancestor's name into a search engine: a surprising number of documents are now being reproduced online, and you could find a reference to your ancestor in a local directory or similar source – it's a long shot, but worth trying, especially if the person you are looking for may have been a vessel owner or fish merchant. Obviously, though, if they had a very common name the chances of finding anything relevant are slim.

1.4 Archives and local studies libraries

At some point, you will almost certainly have to start looking at original documents, which means visiting archives. This might sound daunting and it can be time-consuming and, if you have to make trips away from home, costly. It is also fascinating, and discovering information from documents that in some cases may not have been looked at for many years is very rewarding indeed.

As mentioned above, there is no one core collection of documents relating to the fishing industry, since records are distributed around a variety of repositories. The nearest to a central archive that exist are the Board of Trade archive at the National Archives (www. nationalarchives.gov.uk) in London and the records of the Fishery Board for Scotland, which are held at the National Archives of Scotland in Edinburgh (www.nas.gov.uk). There are also very extensive collections relating to the local fishing industry in the archives of port towns and many coastal counties.

Various general guides to archives are available, such as Janet Foster and Julia Sheppard's *British Archives: A Guide to Archive Resources in the United Kingdom* (Palgrave, 2001) or Christine Morris and Gillian Rayment's *Record Offices: How to Find Them* (Federation of Family History Societies, 2006). However, it is also very easy to find archives online via the A–Z of record repositories, which can be found at www.nationalarchives.gov.uk/archon, and a directory of holdings in archives, libraries and museums can be found at www.nationalarchives.gov.uk/nra. There is also a very useful searchable database giving details of holdings in a great many archives at www.a2a.org.uk, although this is not yet comprehensive.

The National Archives, which you are likely to have to visit at some point, is very large indeed and can seem bewildering at first. However, it is very well organized, the computerized systems for ordering documents are simple once you have got the hang of them, and the staff are invariably helpful. A reader's ticket is necessary if you wish to consult original records, but you can access documents on microfilm without one. Tickets are free, and valid for three years. You can pre-register online but you will need to take two forms of identification with you when you visit, with proof of your identity and address.

On the website there is also an online catalogue. It is a good idea to familiarize yourself with this before visiting, and also some of the numerous research guides that you may find useful. At the time of writing there is none that relates specifically to fishing but there are many for merchant shipping, for which some of the same sources are used. The National Archives also has a very good bookshop, in which you can find most of the source guides mentioned in this book as well as many other general guides to tracing your family history.

Increasingly, many key records are available only on microfilm. Where this is the case with fishing records, it is indicated in the text. Microfilms are consulted in the Open Reading Room, where they are located in cabinets for you to help yourself. There is also an enquiry desk in the Open Reading Room, where staff are available to help out with any queries you might have. Records on microfilm can be more difficult to read than the originals, since it is not possible to hold down the edges of torn pages to identify that crucial but obliterated word, and reading on a screen can be tiring. Copies can be made on the microfilm printing machines for 25p per A3 sheet, although the quality of the printouts can be variable.

The National Archives is by far the largest repository in the United Kingdom. Other archives are invariably much smaller and less sophisticated, in terms of computerized ordering systems and suchlike. Each record office has its own system for cataloguing and managing its collections, although most work along roughly the same principles. An increasing number of archives are now putting their catalogues online. These are rarely as comprehensive as the hard-copy catalogues, but they do at least make it easier to assess whether or not they have enough material to justify a visit. Where catalogues are not online most archives will send photocopies of parts of their hard-copy catalogues, as long as you can give them a clear idea of what you are looking for. Many also produce information sheets on popular subjects, including fisheries records in some places, which are often available to consult online.

It is a good idea to make use of online catalogues and information sheets before visiting so as to cut down the possibility of a wasted journey, and to contact local record offices before you visit since some require you to reserve a seat in their reading rooms. Invariably, as with the National Archives, you will be allowed to use only pencils in the reading rooms, or laptop computers. Most archives will allow you to photograph documents, which is a good idea if you wish to cover a lot of ground in limited time and read through the documents at your leisure, but some will charge a fee. A high-quality camera is essential if you decide to go down this route, and preferably a stand as well. You may not always be permitted to use this, but some places, including the National Archives, provide them.

Another thing to do before you go is to think about the type of

Mending nets on the quayside in the mid-1950s. This picture was taken in France, but similar scenes could be found all around the coasts of Britain. (Basil Greenhill Collection)

documents you will be looking at and make sure you will be able to interpret them. Medieval sources, for instance, are almost invariably in Latin, so a working knowledge of this is essential. Palaeography is another useful skill to acquire, since handwriting from hundreds of years ago can be hard to interpret unless you have had some practice. It is as well to obtain one of the many available primers on palaeography and familiarize yourself with the sort of writing you are likely to encounter. It is also a good idea to familiarize yourself with any technical terms you might come across: a brief glossary can be found in Appendix 3.

When in archives, try to work systematically through your list of documents to consult, and always keep a list of what you have looked at so as to avoid duplicating work if you have to come back. You are also quite likely to find a few things you did not know about beforehand, so try to leave enough time to consult some of these. Original documents are often fascinating even if they do not contain exactly the information you are looking for and it is easy to get side-tracked or end up spending time in interesting blind alleys. It is as well to allow time enough for this too. This last caution also applies to local studies libraries, which are the main repositories for documents such as newspapers and local directories. Local studies libraries are usually attached to larger libraries, and even quite small ones can hold useful collections. Generally they have less of an online presence than archives, but most can be found through local council websites.

If for any reason you are not able to visit archives yourself, professional researchers can undertake research on your behalf, for an hourly or daily fee. Many of these maintain websites and therefore can be found using search engines. Others can be found using local directories, and sometimes advertisements in archives, libraries and family history magazines.

1.5 Basic genealogical sources

Basic genealogical sources such as birth, marriage and death certificates, census returns and wills will not often tell you much about the career of an individual fisherman, but they are well worth consulting as a starting point and a good number can now be consulted online. The indexes are often free to browse, but you will probably have to pay a small subscription fee to view the information relating to an individual. This is well worth doing, since it is likely to cost less than a visit to consult the originals.

1.5.1 Birth, marriage and death records

Since the sixteenth century, births, marriages and deaths have been recorded in parish registers by local clergymen. The survival rate of these is patchy, and few have survived that predate the seventeenth century for England, Wales and Scotland, and the eighteenth century for Ireland. Many of the older registers that still exist have been transferred to county record offices for safe storage. An enquiry to the relevant record office or parish church should confirm what survives and where it can be found. There is also an incomplete index to births and marriages, which can be browsed at www.familysearch.org, and some entries from the National Burial Index can be found at www.familyhistoryonline.co.uk.

National registration of births, marriages and deaths began on 1 July 1837 in England and Wales, 1855 in Scotland and 1864 in Ireland, and the system is still in place in largely the same form today. Indexes to certificates can be found on several websites, such as www.freebmd.org.uk, www.1837online.com and www.familyrelatives.com. A complete set of registers is available at the National Archives, to where records from the Family History Centre have recently been transferred. Certificates can be ordered from there. They can also be ordered online via the General Register Office website (www.gro.gov.uk). At the time of writing, this costs £7 (6.98 in the Republic of Ireland or £10 in Northern Ireland).

The system is different in Scotland. There are no indexes, and birth certificates over fifty years old, marriage certificates seventy-five years old and death certificates 100 years old can be found online at www.scotlandspeople.gov.uk. A complete set can be found at New Register House in Edinburgh (www.gro-scotland.gov.uk). In both cases, you have to pay a fee to view them.

For those tracing ancestors in merchant shipping, there are several sources relating to births, marriages and deaths at sea. Most of these do not apply to the fishing industry. An additional problem exists with tracing the deaths of fishermen, which is that until 1879

Inshore fishing boats in Padstow. Most are local, except the Hull-registered coble in the foreground. (Basil Greenhill Collection)

there was no obligation to report a death aboard a fishing vessel, and even after the law was changed, the practice was probably not followed in all cases. Most who died at sea were taken home for burial, but in the case of someone who was washed overboard or whose vessel sank there was often no body to bury and consequently no record of the death may exist. After 1879, deaths of fishermen may be recorded in the main registers of deaths of seamen, which are held in the National Archives (BT 153 indexed by name in BT 154, or BT 334 after 1890), but this will only cover vessels for which crew lists had to be made out (see Chapter 4), on which deaths at sea were logged. Some isolated records of deaths at sea can be found in parliamentary documents relating to the fishing industry, but these are usually just statistical returns.

1.5.2 The Census

A census has been held in Britain every ten years since 1801 (1821 in Ireland) with the exception of 1941. Before 1841, however, details of individuals were not recorded. Census returns remain closed for 100 years to protect confidential personal information, so the latest that can be consulted at the time of writing is 1901. Under the Freedom of Information Act, the National Archives will now supply limited information from the 2011 census for a fee. An online service will probably become operative in 2009. However, the full census will not become available until 2012.

All the census returns are now online at www.ancestry.co.uk and some on other genealogy sites as well, such as the 1841 census on www.britishorigins.com, and www.1837online.com, which contains the 1861 census. You can browse and search on a name for free on these sites, but you have to pay a subscription to view the full details. The 1901 census can be found on the National Archives website at www.1901census.nationalarchives.gov.uk, where scanned images of the actual census returns can be down-loaded for a fee. The 1881 census can be browsed free at www.familyhistoryonline.co.uk. Hard-copy census records for England and Wales can be consulted at the National Archives, and those for Scotland are at New Register House, or can be found online at www.scotlandspeople.gov.uk. Irish census returns have mostly been destroyed apart from 1901 and 1911: what survives can be found in the National Archives of Ireland. The Dublin census returns for 1911 can be found at www.census.nationalarchives.ie.

Census returns record who was living at a given address on census night, with their full names, ages, occupations and relation-ship to the head of the household. Ships in port, including fishing vessels, were recorded, but those at sea were not, so finding a fisherman in the census can be a hit and miss business (although if you have a home address you can obviously find out about the household your ancestor lived in and who he shared it with). Apart from this, the same tips apply to searching for fishermen as anyone else. It is a good idea to be aware of some of the terminology you are likely to meet before you start searching, especially job titles. Fishermen are normally noted clearly, sometimes with the position they held at the time ('mate', 'deckhand' and suchlike), but there are various terms to describe apprentices ('fisher lad', 'fisherman apprentice' and so on) and occupations on the landward side of the industry can be obscure. It is as well to know what a barker or beatster are before you are confronted by them. Be aware, too, that part-time and seasonal fishermen not actually working as such on census night may be categorized by their other occupations.

1.5.3 Wills

From wills dating as far back as the sixteenth century historians have managed to find information on fishermen's property and businesses that could be found nowhere else, indicating how valuable a resource they can be. However, since a majority of fishermen were men of small means with little property to dispose of, a comparatively small percentage made wills, except for more prosperous fishermen, such as successful trawler skippers, and those who owned their own vessels.

Prior to 1858, wills were proved in a variety of ecclesiastical courts, but most fishermen's wills would probably go through the Archdeacons' courts, which dealt with goods located in one archdeaconry, usually small estates. Larger estates were dealt with in bishop's and archbishop's courts. The records of the most important court, the Prerogative Court of Canterbury, are in the National Archives (classes PROB 1, 10 and 11), whilst others are in local record offices and some are being placed online. Prerogative Court of Canterbury wills can be downloaded for a fee from www.nationalarchives.gov.uk/documentsonline. There is also an index that can search by occupation as well as name.

In 1858, a national system was established whereby wills were granted in local probate registries or the Principal Probate Registry in London. An annual National Probate Index was produced thereafter, which for 1858 to 1946 can be browsed on microfiche in many archives and local studies libraries, including the National Archives. Copies of the wills themselves can be obtained for a fee of £5 from the Probate Registry office in York. This office also holds a copy of the indexes from 1858 to the present day.

Scottish wills from 1500 to 1901 can be browsed at www.scotlandspeople.gov.uk, which also includes a useful guide to reading wills and, indeed, many other basic genealogical resources.

1.5.4 Photographs

Photography was first developed during the second quarter of the nineteenth century, although it was the 1890s before small, easily used cameras with modern film rolls came onto the market. From the late nineteenth century and after, then, many thousands of photographs of fishing vessels and fishermen exist, and give a very vivid picture of life and labour in the fishing industry.

There are several large collections accessible to the public. The National Maritime Museum has very extensive collections, and others exist in local archives and museums. There are also, of course, many private collections, and many old photographs among family papers. Unfortunately, individuals are anonymous in many of them and probably impossible to identify with certainty unless you have another photograph of an individual to compare with, but there are ways in which you can get a much clearer idea of where and when an unidentified photograph – say, one in the possession of a family member – was taken. A very useful guide to dating photographs,

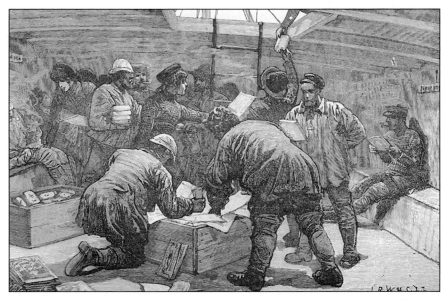

A prayer meeting aboard a Mission to Deep Sea Fishermen smack, in the 1880s.

especially studio portraits, can be found in Robert Pols, *Family Photographs* (Public Record Office, 2002).

The type of photograph, if you can identify it, can help to date a picture. Also, many early professional photographers' pictures include their name, meaning that directories can be used to identify approximately when and where the picture was taken. Beyond that, it is a matter of using the content of the image itself. Geographical features such as buildings, harbours and land formations are obviously useful in identifying places and, when compared with other photographs, can also help to give a rough date, as can other things in the background such as vehicles. The styles of dress of any onlookers may give a rough idea of date, while the dress worn by fishermen in the picture can give a clue as to locality, since styles varied – but you need a very expert eye to spot most of the differences.

If a boat is featured the first thing to look for is a name or a registration. Fishing vessels had to display a port registration number from 1869 onwards: the uses of this are discussed in Chapter 5, and a list of port markings is in Appendix 2. However, many vessels spent part of the year working away from their home ports, and could be transferred permanently whilst retaining their original registration, so port markings do not necessarily tell you where a vessel was photographed.

Visible details of vessels and fishing gear can be very informative, especially for photographs from the nineteenth and early twentieth centuries, when fishing vessel types were more regionally diverse than they are now. Within broad types of ship there were many variations in building practice between different ports and shipyards, and with close attention to detail and reference to some of the more technical books on vessel design – for example, the works of Edgar March on sailing trawlers, drifters and inshore fishing boats, or the excellent *Chatham Directory of Inshore Craft* – it is sometimes possible to identify roughly where a ship was built, although again, many transferred to other places during their lifetimes.

Further Reading

In addition to the many general guides to family history sources on the market, these four books offer particular advice on tracing merchant seamen, although only the second covers fishing records in any depth. In many source guides there are some errors, especially regarding the registration of fishing vessels.

Alison Duffield, *Tracing Your Family History: Merchant Navy* (Imperial War Museum, 2005)

Kelvin Smith, Christopher T and Michael J Watts, *Records of Merchant Shipping and Seamen* (Public Record Office, 1998)

Christopher T and Michael J Watts, *My Ancestor Was a Merchant Seaman* (2nd edn, Society of Genealogists, 2002)

Christopher T & Michael J Watts, *Tracing Births, Deaths and Marriages at Sea* (Society of Genealogists, 2004)

Chapter Two

THE MEDIEVAL FISHERIES

Fishing is one of the oldest activities pursued by mankind, predating settled agriculture. No doubt some of the earliest inhabitants of the British Isles sought fish in the rivers and estuaries, and later in the sea close inshore. By classical times there was an extensive and highly organized fishing industry in the Mediterranean. Fish was evidently not widely eaten in Ancient Greece, but the Romans caught tuna and sea fish such as mackerel and snapper, and thousands of slaves were trained as fishermen, some of them working in oyster-farming, which the Romans turned into a systematic and comparatively large-scale industry. A division which to an extent persists to the present emerged between high- and low-class fish consumption, with scarce and expensive fresh fish being eaten by the wealthy and large quantities of fish being preserved by salting for consumption by the poor. How far this affected northern Europe is open to question. The population there was smaller and less dense, and the seas rougher. There was still extensive subsistence fishing, though, and by the seventh century trade in fish, mainly herring, had become established. The Vikings and Normans are credited with the first ventures into deeper waters, mainly fishing for herring in the North Sea and, later, off the coast of southern Ireland.

Towns played an important role in establishing the fish trades and encouraging the catching effort, since they acted as centres for trade in cured fish and necessaries such as salt and barrels. London had a Fishmongers' Company from 1154, which became one of the city's most powerful livery companies, setting rules on the sale of fish and settling disputes among its members in private courts. The Fishmongers' Company still exists, although far more limited in its powers. The Hanseatic League, an association of north German ports which from the thirteenth century extended its influence across northern Europe, came to control much of the North Sea trade in herrings, as well as the all-important supply of salt for preserving them. The fish trades became a complex business, with a limited amount sold directly by fishermen and the majority handled by merchants and curers. 'Rippiers' were specialized retailer-transporters who purchased fish at the coast and marketed it inland. They evidently played an important role in provisioning London from the coasts of Kent and Essex, but they were active all over the country. Many would sell all or part of their wares on to local fishmongers. Some general merchants also involved them-

Image from the Tacuinum Sanitatis, *a medieval treatise on health. Like most medieval depictions of fishing, it is heavily stylized.*

selves in the fish supply chain in addition to dealing in other commodities, especially in the larger towns with good access to major roads.

Local authorities took a hand in controlling the trade from an early stage, both because it was a source of revenue and because fish is a perishable and potentially antisocial commodity. Many rules, such as those at Scarborough in the fourteenth century banning fishermen from hanging fish up in the streets to dry, were aimed at mitigating the smell and mess caused by the trade. Others, such as strict rules on selling oysters in thirteenth-century London, aimed to prevent the sale of decaying fish. Others still sought to prevent sharp practices in the marketplace by setting rules on weights and measures, and banning activities such as 'forestalling', buying up fish before it reached the market to sell it again later at a high price.

Overlaying all of this was the authority of the Catholic Church and its fasting practices, which reinforced the importance of fish to the medieval diet. The origins of these lay back in the fourth century, and by 1300 meat was not to be eaten in Lent, at Advent, on Wednesdays, Fridays and Saturdays, or on the eve of feast days. Consequently, the laity was expected to abstain from meat for nearly half the year. Coupled with a rising population and pressure on land, this encouraged the consumption of fish to increase: it appears to have reached a high point in the first half of the fourteenth century.

By 1300, then, the British Isles possessed fisheries and fish trades of considerable size and sophistication. Our information on this is fragmentary – an estimate of numbers of boats working here, an account of tithes and taxes paid there – and information on fishing for subsistence alone is very sparse indeed. At this stage, in fact, there are probably more records relating to trade in fish and related goods than there are relating to the catching effort. It seems clear enough, however, that the growth and expansion of the earlier medieval period came to an end in the second half of the fourteenth century, at least on the east coast, and that the following century saw more activity and some key developments in western England.

The herring was the most commercially important species. It was thought that herring shoals circulated clockwise around the coasts of Britain, gathering off north and west Scotland in spring and early summer, off Yorkshire in the summer, East Anglia in autumn and the south-west in the winter. Only recently has it been discovered that there is no one constantly circling, population but several, arriving off the British coast at different times. Fishermen caught herring with nets – the drift net was introduced in the fifteenth century – when they were in season, and either worked on the land or targeted cod and other demersal fish with lines and traps, or gathered shellfish at other times. This seasonal pattern regulated by the fish available continues to the present day. Much fishing was primarily for subsistence, but herring fishing also sustained livelihoods and trading connections all over Europe.

The fisheries of the east coast were generally larger-scale and more commercial at this time, and encompassed major centres of trade such as Scarborough and Great Yarmouth. Here, annual 'herring fairs' coincided with the catching season and attracted large numbers of visitors from the continent and from elsewhere in the British Isles. In 1342–3, about 500 visiting boats paid 'murage' dues at Yarmouth. The fairs also attracted visiting traders, 'hosted' by local merchants who provided accommodation and commercial contacts, but also made sure that the interlopers did not encroach on their own businesses. Some merchants owned fishing vessels and employed crews, but more were probably owned by their skippers or by others. For example, Alan Seamer of Scarborough owned three vessels in 1336, from which he probably made a comfortable living, although profits from fishing were always unpredictable. Some larger 'farcosta' vessels were used, but most fishing boats were open craft no larger than ten or twenty tons, rigged with a simple square sail but navigated mainly under oars by their crews of five or six. They fished within a few miles of the shore, staying out for no more than a night at a stretch.

The west coast fishery was more dispersed and smaller scale. The population was sparser, there were fewer large towns and the terrain was more difficult, so access to markets for fish of all sorts was more problematic. Meanwhile, the herrings were less abundant and in Wales, especially, the volatile political situation deterred landowners and merchants from investing in fishing and disrupted activity. Even so, there was still a substantial herring fishery in north Wales, and all along the west coast there was extensive fishing with weirs, or 'Goredi' as they were known. Weirs were simple affairs of stone and brushwood, set across rivers and in channels built on the beaches, which simply trapped fish behind them as the tide receded, after which they could be extracted with small nets or even by hand. This was a way of supplementing the peasants' diet, if not of catching enough to sell.

The situation changed in the mid-fourteenth century, with the east coast fisheries entering a period of difficulty and sometimes decline. The first cause was the Black Death, the bubonic plague which in its first and most notorious outbreak in 1349 may have killed a third of the population. Subsequent outbreaks were not as devastating, but even so the population growth of the previous few centuries ground to a halt, with serious economic implications. Port towns, where the plague entered the country, were especially hard hit, and although fishing and trade were often conducted from separate places, towns such as Scarborough and Great Yarmouth did both and their fishing interests were certainly damaged by the plague. The long period of wars known as the Hundred Years' War broke out in 1337, and turned French and Flemish fishermen into enemy aliens rather than profitable visitors to the herring fairs. War also disrupted exports, and although large quantities of herring were purchased to feed the armies – in 1338, Edward III obtained from Yarmouth forty lasts of herrings (about half a million fish) to feed his army in Flanders – this certainly did not compensate for the disruption and loss of markets. Perhaps more important than war was competition from foreign fishermen, especially the Dutch, to whose economy herring was especially important. Amsterdam, the saying went, was built on a foundation of herring bones. In the fifteenth century a substantial sum of money was invested in developing the fishery, which became highly successful and managed to shut exports from England and Scotland out of important markets. Disturbed by war, plague and competition, the British fishery contracted. Exports from Yarmouth, for example, fell from more than 500 lasts a year in mid-century to less than 100 by 1400, and stagnation continued well into the fifteenth century.

The west coast fared rather better, and its comparatively slow growth to date gave way in the fifteenth century to a period of

Hauling in drift nets from an open boat. This nineteenth-century drawing depicts a scene that had changed little for centuries.

expansion and innovation. This was especially the case in the south-west, which had the advantages of improving trading connections both inland and by sea, a broad-based economy encompassing fishing and mining in addition to agriculture, and abundant fishing grounds for a variety of species close inshore. The fishing interests of Cornwall, in particular, grew markedly at this time.

One key development was the pilchard fishery. Pilchards are a shoaling fish quite similar to herring, and in fact at this time were sometimes taken to be herrings, some contemporary comments referring to 'herring called pilchards'. They could be found off the Cornish coast all year round and were sometimes caught with drift nets, but in autumn and summer vast shoals of them came close inshore, where they were caught in large seines. These were anchored on shore at one end, and then a boat towed the other end around to encircle the shoal, its movements directed by a 'huer' on the cliff top who watched the movement of the shoal and signalled to the boats with flags and hand signals. Once the shoal was trapped, the whole seine was hauled into shallow water and the fish extracted with small 'tuck' nets and taken off for curing. Seining took off in the fifteenth century as a new method of curing was developed, a combination of dry-salting followed by washing and packing the pilchards into barrels, pressing them down with a weight to squeeze out the oil, before repacking. The pilchards thus produced kept better than those subjected to previous means of preservation. This method also created a valuable by-product, the oil known as 'train oil', which was used for lighting. Fourteen cargoes of pilchards left the West Country in 1492–3, most of them bound for the Mediterranean, especially Italy.

Shellfish were caught all around the coasts of the British Isles. Most were food for the poor, cockles and mussels raked up by hand and sold cheaply, while oysters were also cheap and plentiful enough to be eaten by those of modest means. Oyster fisheries were more highly organized than most, since the beds where oysters were

Handling a seine on the beach. This method, used mainly for taking pilchards, was developed in medieval times, and continued until the early twentieth century. (Basil Greenhill Collection)

fattened and dredged from were close inshore and the rights to fish on them were granted by the authorities. The Borough Charter of Colchester from 1189 gave the burgesses of the town the right to fish for oysters in the Colne estuary, and a company was set up to administer the fishery and adjudicate in disputes between fishermen, of which there were many. Oysters still went cheap, though: in London in 1491 they were four pence per bushel. Crabs and lobsters, however, were caught in much smaller quantities and were the preserve of the wealthy. When William of Wykeham entertained Richard II in 1393, he paid 25s 8d for thirty-three crabs, a rate far above the average person's means.

White fish were pursued all around the coast, often in seasonal rotation with herring, although there were already some who specialized in catching them. Hake was caught in large quantities off the south-west, although much was also imported. Fishermen in the north sought cod, haddock and ling for consumption locally, and also for salting or drying for sale. Most was caught close inshore by men of small means, working with hand-lines and various forms of traps. There was, however, some experimental fishing by other means including a controversial device used in the shallow parts of the Thames estuary. It was known as the wondyrchoun, and consisted of a bag-shaped net kept open by a beam of wood and dragged along the bottom, scooping up fish as went. In other words, a small and primitive version of the trawl was already in use, until it was banned in 1376 because of the quantities of small and immature fish it caught, 'to the great damage of the Commons of the Realm and the destruction of the fisheries'. Overfishing is not a new problem, and nor are regulations which attempt to prevent it. There was evidently some resistance to the law, for in 1406 there was a riot in Barking when an inspector seized some illegal nets, which the fishermen then turned out in force to seize back. The ringleaders were tried, but let off on condition that the illegal nets be publicly burned.

The boats were mainly open craft of much the same type as those used for herring, but there was already a movement towards fishing in more distant waters, which required larger and more seaworthy vessels. These were still single-masted boats, but rudders began to replace steering oars from the early fourteenth century, and navigation became more exact as compasses began to come into use, allowing for longer voyages. That said, for many centuries thereafter fishermen were renowned for making long passages and knowing their whereabouts precisely without the assistance of even quite basic navigational aids. Some of the larger vessels evidently also had wells, sections of the hull sealed off from the rest and pierced to allow seawater to circulate, so fish, especially cod, could be kept alive and therefore fresh inside.

Fishing in the North Sea shaded off into activity in more distant waters. The seas around the Shetland Islands were regularly fished, and from the late fourteenth century there are references to boats working in northern waters. Norfolk men are noted as having fished the Norwegian coast in the 1380s, but pressure from the Hanseatic League made ports such as Bergen less hospitable, and by 1413 thirty English ships were reported working off Iceland, a number which grew in subsequent years. Fishing off Iceland was a major undertaking, and merchants from trading ports such as Hull and Bristol invested substantially in it. Vessels from East Anglian ports

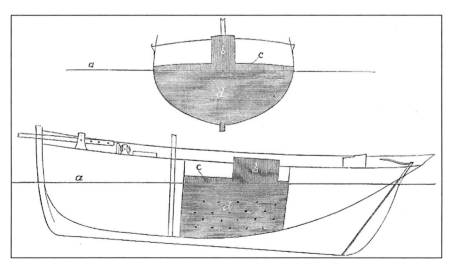

Diagram of a nineteenth-century well smack, showing how part of the hull was flooded to keep fish alive.

also featured prominently. The vessels were two-masted craft known as 'doggers' or 'droghers', and were comparatively large vessels capable of carrying about fifteen lasts – thirty tons – of dried cod, termed stockfish. They were crewed by five or ten men. They sailed in the spring, often carrying goods outward for sale in Iceland. Once they arrived, the men set up shore bases with space to dry and pack the catch, which was taken with hand-lines from small boats. This continued until autumn, when the bases were dismantled and the vessels returned home. This was an unusually dangerous activity, since the waters around Iceland were not well known at this time and the climate was very harsh. A storm in 1419 caused the loss of twenty-five vessels, many of them evidently from Scarborough, which may well have caused a partial withdrawal of that port from the Iceland fishery. This was a particularly serious incident, but small numbers of vessels were lost on a more or less regular basis. The potential rewards made the risks worthwhile, however, and as late as 1481 thirteen vessels from Dunwich alone went to Iceland.

This level of activity led to friction with the Icelanders from an early stage, an official there complaining in 1425 that the English fishermen monopolized the Reykanes Peninsula, and 'made use of everything as if it was their own'. There were periodic scuffles between locals and visitors, and the Danish government – Iceland then being a dependency of Denmark – tried to restrict English participation in the fishery. Fishing was theoretically forbidden altogether for a year in 1415, although the means of enforcing this were small and some fishing almost certainly continued. An edict of 1420, which aimed to control trade in Iceland by setting fixed prices for fish in relation to other goods – three fish being equal to one pair of women's shoes, for instance – was little more successful. In 1490 an Anglo-Danish treaty removed the restrictions on English visitors to Iceland, by which time the English were dominant in the fishery.

Although medieval fishing was a minor activity by modern standards, by those of the day it was a large and complex business, and surprisingly modern in may respects. Direct seigniorial, 'feudal', control of fishing certainly existed. In the same way as peasant farmers, villeins were obliged to work a certain number of

Representation of a large fishing vessel of the fifteenth century, probably a buss.
(Mariner's Mirror 3 *(1913),* reproduced by kind *permission of the editor)*

days annually on their lords' lands; this meant that in some coastal areas villeins were obliged to fish, and in many places landlords issued licences to fish and claimed the right of first purchase over what was caught. Nevertheless, the most important areas of activity, among them the great herring fisheries and the Icelandic cod fishery, were already capitalistic businesses producing a commodity that was marketed via international trading networks. The processes that were to shape the fishing industry in the future were already well under way.

2.1 Manorial records

The word 'manor' tends to make us think of elegant country houses, but in fact it has three meanings. It can refer to the residence of a landowner, which today is how we tend to use it. Secondly, it can refer to an area of land which might or might not contain the landowner's home and over which he exercised control, including seigniorial rights over any tenants. This definition is the one that most concerns us, since the manor was one of the main units of local administration in medieval England and parts of Wales, mainly the areas colonized by the Normans such as the Vale of Glamorgan, the Gower and parts of the Cardigan coast. It is not known how many manors there were in England and Wales: estimates range from 25,000 to 65,000. They were not coterminous with parishes, of which there were roughly 12,000: many parishes encompassed more than one manor, and some manors included parts of more than one parish. Finally, the 'manor' can refer to a piece of land with tenants over whom the landlord had rights of jurisdiction in a private, manorial, court. Obviously, these three definitions overlap, but the distinction is useful because they become more or less accurate over time. The first definition is how we think of a manor today, the second is usually most accurate for the thirteenth to fifteenth centuries, and after the mid-sixteenth only the third applies. Most manors can roughly be divided into two components: the tenements, parcels of land worked by tenants, and the demesne, which was reserved for the use of the lord.

Records from coastal manors have been much used by historians of medieval fisheries, since they can allow you to assess if any fishing was being conducted from the manor and, if so, what and how extensive it was. They can also tell you what obligations the tenants of the manor had to the landlord. For instance, the records of Stokenham, South Devon, show that the villeins were obliged to fish for mullet from early February to the week after Easter. The lord took one-third of the catch, and also claimed the right to purchase any valuable bycatch such as salmon, rays and cod. Most of the research that has already been done relates to the West Country and many areas have barely been researched, making manorial records a potentially valuable source of new information. While there are tenant lists for certain manors, in most cases it will not be possible to identify individuals, unless there was some particular reason for them to appear in the records, such as a dispute they were involved in coming before the manorial court.

The survival rate of manorial documents is variable, but improves over time. A random survey of manors in five counties suggests that for one-third there are no documents at all, and records from the fifteenth century and earlier exist for only around one in twenty-five. For about a fifth there are runs of records from the sixteenth and seventeenth centuries, and for over half after this.

Manorial records, like most others, become more detailed as time goes on. Early ones are usually very sparse, but later ones can be a mine of information. Broadly, the records fall into two main types. First, there are the records of the estate, consisting of surveys and accounts. Surveys are written descriptions (very few maps were made) of the property belonging to the manor, such as farmland, mills and, in some cases, fisheries, either in rivers passing through the manor or in the seas adjoining it. If the lord claimed the right to issue licences to fish, then this will be noted. Very occasionally, it might be possible to find the names of those who held licences. Surveys may also contain a description of the obligations that tenants owed to the lord, which can include fishing for a set number of days, or at a particular time of the year. Meanwhile, the accounts show what the manor produced, how much of it and what money was raised by selling it. Again, this can include fish. Secondly, the

A Somerset Flatner, used for fishing around the mudflats of the Bristol Channel.
(Basil Greenhill Collection)

records of manorial courts give details of matters that came before them, such as transfers of land and, perhaps most usefully, any disputes between and misdemeanours committed by the tenants. Cornwall Record Office, for example, has some court records relating to fishing dating from the fifteenth century and after, including disputes and inquiries into fishery rights in a few coastal manors.

Very few manorial documents have been published, so you are likely to have to use original documents, which can be found in a variety of places. A few remain with the institutions that created them, such as cathedral priories. Some, especially where lands were taken over by the state for some reason, are in the National Archives or British Library. Most are to be found in local record offices. Until recently, these could be hard to track down, but the National Archives has now established a Manorial Documents Register, which can be found online at www.nationalarchives.gov.uk/mdr. It is not complete at the time of writing, but will be a very valuable resource. There is also an excellent page on manorial records in the north-west, maintained by the University of Lancaster at www. lancs.ac.uk/fass/projects/manorialrecords. The usual archive search engines will also return results.

Most of the remarks about other medieval records apply to using manorial documents but a very useful introductory guide with a comprehensive links page can be found at www.medieval genealogy.org.uk/sources/manorial.shtml. The best book giving a full-length introduction to manorial documents is P D A Harvey's *Manorial Records* (British Records Association, revised edition 1999). *Manorial Records* by Denis Stuart (Phillimore, 1992) is a very useful primer for those intending to look at original records, since it gives copies from actual documents, giving you some idea what to expect, and some idea of the level of Latin and palaeography skills you will need. Latin ceased formally to be used only in 1734, but there are many documents in English from before then.

2.2 Tithe records

Tithes were payments by parishioners of a proportion of the profits from farming and other activities for the upkeep and support of the parish church and clergy. They can roughly be divided into two types. 'Great tithes' include 'predial' and 'mixed' tithes on crops and livestock, and 'small tithes' the 'personal' tithes on the produce of man's labour, including milling and, most significantly for us, fishing.

Originally, tithes were payments in kind (hence the existence of 'tithe barns', where the goods were stored), but from an early date money payments began to be made instead, and this accelerated with land enclosures, especially from the eighteenth century, at which time tithes were often reassessed and in-kind tithes replaced with a fixed or variable charge. By the Tithe Commutation Act of 1836, all great tithes in England and Wales were commuted to a money payment. This did not, however, apply to personal tithes, including those on fish. Tithes were modified by several other Acts of Parliament over the next century, and effectively abolished in 1936, when they were converted into annuities payable by landowners to the government. This scheme was finally wound up in 1977.

In general, there are far fewer records relating to tithes on fishing than on farming, but material does exist, and historians of medieval fisheries have used tithe records quite extensively. Accounts of tithes paid are a valuable source of information on what fishing took place in an area and how extensive and profitable it was. Less use has been made of later tithe records, which offer plenty of scope for research, although the likelihood of finding an individual is comparatively small. The right to collect tithes could be leased out, and many such leases and deeds can be found in local archives.

The largest collection of records relating to the tithe is in the National Archives, but much of this consists of surveys made for the Commutation Act and has little relevance to the fisheries researcher. Many tithe records can be found in church archives. For example Exeter Cathedral Library has tithe accounts for some places in Devon dating back to medieval times. Apart from this, county archives hold a wide variety of material, most of it postdating the medieval period. Cornwall Record Office, for example, has numerous papers relating to disputes over tithes, receipts for tithe fish and the odd account book dating from the seventeenth and eighteenth centuries. If you wish to find out in details about holdings of tithe records relating to fishing, it is best to write directly to the archives.

Tithes in fish were technically payable in some places until 1936, but in most instances were not collected and little information on them appears to have survived.

2.3 Port books and customs records

Customs and port records are generally concerned with trade rather than fishing, but they can still be of some use. In the first instance, the information they contain is of interest to anyone trying to research the fisheries of a particular area, which is how they have mainly been used by historians. Secondly, they name individual ships and their masters, which can include fishing vessels when these were also used seasonally for trading, as many were until the sixteenth and seventeenth centuries. There is, then, some limited scope for tracing individuals, although with the caveat that since they relate mainly to a time before ships were registered it is often not possible to be sure that a fishing vessel and trading ship with the same name were one and the same.

Customs records have been kept since 1272, for the purposes of recording duties paid by ships trading abroad. Since herring was a staple of north European trade, barrelled, cured herring can be found frequently, although often as part-cargoes with various other goods. Customs accounts from 1272 to 1565 are in the National Archives in class E 122, arranged by port. The content is rather varied, but typically includes the name of ship and master, name of the merchant shipping the goods, a description of the cargo, its origin and destination and any duty paid (coastal vessels did not pay duty). These early customs records come on large scrolls and many have been restored and are therefore in surprisingly good condition. They are, of course, written in Latin.

Port Books proper start from 1565, when the Customs were reformed. They are in class E 190 at the National Archives, arranged

Late thirteenth-century customs account for the port of Scarborough.
(The National Archives, E122/55/6)

by port and by the different types of customs official who kept them. A research guide to the Port Books is available for download from the National Archives website. They contain much the same information as the previous records, albeit with more detail on the ship's tonnage and suchlike. They run up to the end of the eighteenth century, although the books for many ports stop well before that and there are many gaps. Many are in a poor state of preservation. Similar records for Scottish ports can be found in the National Archives of Scotland in E 71 (up to 1640), E 72 (1661–1696) and E 504 (1742–1830). Some port books for particular ports (for instance, London, Boston and Southampton) and periods have been transcribed and published.

A connected set of records for a later period that can be worth a look are general Customs records. Here, it might be useful to define a Customs Port, since these were where much of the information and many of the sources used in this volume were originally generated. A statute of 1559 divided the coastline of England and Wales into Customs Ports, each administered by a Collector of Customs based in the principal, or 'head' port in the region. Therefore, one Customs Port usually consisted of one large and several smaller ports, and it was at the head port that vessels were registered and customs duties collected. The system was extended to Scotland after the Act of Union in 1707, although the Scottish Board of Customs remained separate, and survived in much modified form until the last century. Therefore, if you are researching fishermen from a very small fishing port, any relevant Customs records will usually be found among those for a much larger port nearby.

Customs records are very extensive and rather miscellaneous, containing numerous documents generated by all aspects of Customs business. The registers of shipping are described in Chapter 5, but there are also minutes of business, books of letters containing various types of business, ranging from apprenticeships to disputes and sometimes registers of apprentices. These last have usually been retained by local Customs Houses and are in the relevant county archives, although those for Scarborough, Ramsgate, Fowey, Bideford, Newhaven, Teignmouth and the Scilly Isles are held in the National Archives. Most of the records for London were destroyed by fire in 1814, but those from after this date are in the

National Archives, as are records for other ports from the late seventeenth to mid-twentieth centuries. Those from England and Wales are in CUST 50, Isle of Man in CUST 104, Channel Islands in CUST 105 and Ireland in CUST 113. The central administrative records of the Scottish Board of Customs are in the National Archives of Scotland, and port records in the relevant local archives.

Further Reading

M Smylie, *Herring: A History of the Silver Darlings* (Tempus, 2004)
D J Starkey, C Reid, C and N Ashcroft, *England's Sea Fisheries: The Commercial Sea Fisheries of England and Wales since 1300* (Chatham, 2000)

Chapter Three

THE BRITISH FISHERIES 1500–1815

In the late fifteenth century, many among the political classes regarded the state of English maritime industries, including the fisheries, with concern. It was felt that they were in no condition to meet competition from the well organized fisheries of the Dutch and Scots. The sixteenth century saw the first of many attempts to improve the fisheries by the action of the state, which continued into the seventeenth and eighteenth centuries, by which time the British economy was seeing growth and development quite independent of any action taken by government.

Fishing may not have been a large industry but it was politically important, in an age when connections between economic strength and effective government were beginning to be understood. Fishermen were useful, in that they could be used to man the navy in wartime, fishing could soak up some of the unemployed labourers who so concerned contemporaries, and exports of fish generated valuable revenue. The Reformation spelled the end for Catholic fasting practices that had formerly encouraged the eating of fish on non-meat days and threatened to harm the fisheries, and to counter this threat a range of statutes enforced the eating of fish on 152 days of the year, somewhat cynically dubbed 'Political Lent', with the aim of encouraging the fisheries. Other measures, such as the Association for the Fishing, set up in 1632 to compete with the Dutch at catching herring in the North Sea, were generally short-lived and unsuccessful.

Inshore fishing, practised all around the coast, was still more or less a subsistence activity in many places, or at best produced only a small surplus for the market. Fishing activity was, as in previous centuries, limited principally by the species available locally, and the ability to market them once caught. As in the fifteenth century, this meant that fishing was particularly active and innovative in the south-west. The seine fishery thrived, despite a brief controversy in 1583 when hostile Spanish troops were said to be feasting on Cornish pilchards, and as international trade grew in general, so did exports. By the late eighteenth century, 90 per cent of pilchard exports went to Italy. Pilchard fishing took over the lives of several small Cornish towns during the brief season. Men came from the farms to man the seines, and whole families took part in the curing. Later, it was said that in St Ives the smell was strong enough to stop the church clock. The hake fishery, meanwhile, stagnated. A survey in 1566 found only three hake nets in Cornwall, the rest mainly

Luggers in Newquay harbour, circa 1900. (Basil Greenhill Collection)

being seines and drift nets for the mackerel fishing. Men moved between the three, and between ports and agricultural work, as demand dictated. The fisheries of the West Country, however, did well throughout most of this period, and by the end of the eighteenth century Cornwall had a large fleet of luggers fishing for mackerel and pilchards. Some Cornish boats, as well as many from the south and east coasts of England, also had a profitable sideline as smuggling vessels, since they were fast enough to outrun the revenue cutters.

Development around most of the country was steady, if not spectacular. On much of the Welsh coast, where fishing was comparatively unimportant and conducted seasonally and on a small scale, the dual economy of fishing and farming prevailed. Elsewhere, fishing was becoming more specialized as it grew. By the eighteenth century, the twenty or so fishing stations on the Yorkshire coast were mainly dedicated fishing centres. Although larger vessels were used for deep-sea fishing, much was caught inshore from cobles, a distinctive local type of vessel with a high prow for seaworthiness and a very flat stern for landing stern-first on the beach.

These Yorkshire fishing villages, like many others around the country, were tight-knit communities dominated by fishing. The labour involved the whole family. Whilst the men went to sea, women and children repaired nets or baited long-lines, gathered shellfish for bait and sometimes even sold the catch, hawking it around neighbouring towns on foot. It was a hard and sometimes precarious life which involved constant hard work for uncertain rewards. Partly because of this and partly because of the isolation of many small fishing villages, communities were self-contained and self-sufficient, each one distinctive from the next in the details of vessels and fishing gear used, in style of dress, in customs and superstitions. Men married girls from within the community or, at furthest, from another fishing port: marrying a girl who knew little of fishing and the work she would have to perform was regarded as a risk. The closeness and insularity of many fishing communities helped people to deal with the physical risks involved in fishing. Few bereaved families were allowed to become destitute, as family, neighbours and friends rallied around to provide support and practical help. Tragedy was a frequent occurrence and, as many a fishwife, haggling with a buyer over her husband's catch is said to have remarked, 'It's not fish you're buying: it's men's lives!'

Fishermen's womenfolk and itinerant sellers known in Cornwall as 'Jowsters' sold parcels of fish inland well into the twentieth century, but well before this many relatively small communities, those not too isolated at least, were becoming linked into a distribution system of growing size and complexity. The most sought-after fish from the Yorkshire coast, principally soles, were sold as far west as Manchester, taken there overnight by packhorse, packed in wet grass to keep them as cool as possible. The quantities were small and the fish was expensive and often none too fresh by the time it arrived, but even so, as the eighteenth century wore on more and more fish reached affluent consumers inland. Poorer people, if they could obtain fresh fish at all, made do with what was too old to sell to the wealthy, which was, to quote a contemporary, 'generally half-rotten and consequently most unwholesome and disgusting food'.

Cured herring was a food of the urban poor, although the greater part of what was produced was exported. The British herring fishery was in the doldrums in the early seventeenth century, although herring was still the most important species caught. The Dutch had introduced the herring buss in the late fifteenth century, and over the next hundred years they developed a highly organized trade in herring. Vessels were licensed, and fished in the North Sea in set places at specified times, starting off in eastern Scotland in the spring and moving down the coast with the herring shoals until the autumn. They worked in fleets, remaining at sea for the whole season with fresh supplies brought out and the cured herring taken to market by cutter. There were strict rules on the size and type of fish that could be cured, the salt and barrels used and the method of gutting and packing the catch. This ensured that Dutch herrings acquired a reputation for consistent high quality that gave them an edge in key export markets.

The British herring fishery was not so successful. Although in 1614 Tobias Gentleman blamed 'slothfulness', it was more the lack of organization and capital that caused lack of success. The stringent rules that gave the Dutch cure its reputation did not exist, and since

A drifter riding to her nets. Note the lowered mainmast and the white light on top of the crutch supporting it. Drifters were supposed to display a light when fishing to warn trawlers to keep clear, although not all did.

fishing was not nearly as important to the British economy as to the Dutch, the political will to create them was absent. Herring fishing, always seasonal, was mainly conducted on a comparatively small scale by communities who engaged in other fisheries out of season, and most herring was caught close inshore from open boats.

The Yorkshire coast was one of a few exceptions to this. Cobles were owned jointly among their crews and used for inshore fishing, generally herring-netting, lining and potting for crabs and lobsters according to the season. They were supplemented by larger 'five-man boats'. These were three-masted, decked luggers, usually part-owned by their crews, with some shares held by local investors – often tradesmen or wealthier farmers. The herring fishery off the Yorkshire coast was declining, and by the end of the eighteenth century was only of local importance, but the 'five-man boats' went to East Anglia for the autumn fishing, and in spring many were used for long-lining for cod on the Dogger Bank. A few continued to work into the early twentieth century.

Scotland and East Anglia were the main centres of the herring trade, and in some places this dominated the economy. In season,

Luggers jostle with coastal sailing ships in this busy drawing of Scarborough harbour in the late nineteenth century. Note the barrels on the quayside, probably filled with herrings ready for export. (Mariner's Mirror 19 (1933))

perhaps two-thirds of adult men at Lowestoft worked in the herring fishery or related occupations. Boats were worked on a system of payment by shares, or 'doles' as they were termed locally, although after 1730 some owners switched to paying their crews at least a basic weekly wage, or an agreed amount per last of herrings caught. A successful herring fishing was a useful supplement to the income of many agricultural labourers who signed on for the season after the harvest was in. In fact, the peak time of year for marriages in Lowestoft was between November and January, in the comparatively prosperous few months after the fishing had finished. For the full-time fishermen, the remainder of the year was spent lining for cod and other demersal fish, as well as a brief early-summer drift-net fishery for mackerel. Lucrative the fishing may have been, but it was also dangerous. During the 1716 season, ten men are known to have drowned at Lowestoft alone, and there were not infrequent references in the parish burial registers to the bodies of nameless strangers, washed ashore.

Late medieval fishing craft such as the crayer, which could be used both for fishing and coastal trading, were dying out in favour of more specialized and larger types of boat. Many of these were owned by local merchants and tradesmen, such as grocers and victuallers. They were supplemented by a larger number of small open 'beach boats', usually owned among their crews of two or three. In addition to developments in the type of boats used, fishing gear was also changing, with nets becoming generally larger and more effective – and as a result catches rose.

The early seventeenth century was a difficult period for the herring fishery in East Anglia, and to an extent for fisheries elsewhere, especially on the east coast. Numbers of vessels and men seem to have fallen, and presumably catches also dropped. Ongoing competition from the Dutch herring fishery, then at its peak, was the main reason for this. Lack of organization, especially on the curing side, the English Civil War and outbreaks of plague in 1603 and 1635

Great Yarmouth herring luggers putting to sea, mid-nineteenth century.

also played some part. From the 1670s, however, the East Anglian fishery recovered, and by 1698 there were thirty-seven 'great boats' fishing, and through the following century the fishery grew further, despite occasional downturns and the impact of successive wars.

The Scottish fishery was more dynamic still, and less vulnerable to disruption in wartime. Moreover, the Union of Scotland and England in 1707 gave it greater access to English markets. Even so, it lagged well behind the Dutch. This gave rise to various attempts on the part of the state to stimulate the industry by offering bounties to fishermen. This happened in England in 1705 and 1718, and then in Scotland in 1727 and, under the aegis of the Society of the Free British Fishery, in 1749. There were also private initiatives, such as the British Fisheries Society, established in 1786. None of these schemes was very successful, because nothing was done to address the problem of variable and sometimes poor curing standards, which made marketing the product difficult. Most of them aimed at emulating the Dutch method of curing fish at sea, despite the fact that Scotland's closeness to the main fishing grounds made it possible to use smaller and cheaper vessels than the busses, and bring the catch ashore for processing. However, bounties helped to stimulate the catching effort, especially after bounties on the finished product replaced those on vessels in 1785, and in 1808, the problem of curing was finally solved. Under the control of the Fishery Board for Scotland, a system was introduced whereby barrels of cured herrings were inspected by an official of the newly founded Fishery Board, and given a brand according to the type and quality of fish. The brand was intended to function as a guarantee of quality, and in this it was largely successful. The defeat of the Dutch in successive wars in the second half of the seventeenth century and rising exports helped to give the British herring fisheries a lead that they held for a century thereafter.

Distant-water fishing for cod increased in importance in the sixteenth and seventeenth centuries, as navigation became more precise, new fishing grounds were opened up and vessels became larger and more seaworthy. The vessels used in previous years were replaced during the seventeenth century with busses, around seventy-five feet long and broadly similar to those used for herring fishing. Iceland remained an important fishing area, with 149 'barks' going there in 1528. Hull was still heavily involved, and along with other ports, such as Grimsby, offered bounties to fishermen to encourage them to base themselves at the port. Further south, Tobias Gentleman could point to the success of places such as Walberswick, Dunwich and Southwold in the Icelandic fisheries as a model for others to follow.

The Iceland boats sailed in the early summer and returned in the autumn. Between times, men had to share one or two cramped cabins, living on a diet composed largely of fish and salt meat and catching fish with hand-lines. It was an uncomfortable life, working in a cold and inhospitable climate. It was also a continuing source of friction with Denmark; and it was dangerous. In the seventeenth century, it was also disrupted by competition from Dutch busses, sent there to catch cod in the off-season for herring, and by the English Civil War.

The cod fisheries recovered in the eighteenth century, but Iceland

Children and rowing boats share space with fishing boats on a West Country beach, probably before the First World War. (Basil Greenhill Collection)

declined as a fishing ground in favour of the North Sea, and the busses were replaced by sleeker and faster fore-and-aft rigged decked boats known as 'smacks'. By 1770, there were more than sixty of them working from Harwich, which was growing fast as a fishing port. They worked mainly on and around the Dogger Bank, fishing with hand-lines in the summer and long-lines during the winter. Many of the largest smacks had wells to bring the last fish caught back to port alive. When they were to be sold, they were taken from cages in the harbour and killed with a blow to the head, giving those involved in this trade the nickname of 'codbangers'.

The other growth area for British distant-water fishing was Newfoundland. The fishing grounds here had been discovered in 1497 by John Cabot, who remarked that it was possible to dip a bucket into the water and bring up fish, so many were there to catch. 'The sea there,' he said, 'is swarming with fish … [and] … that they could bring so many fish that this Kingdom would have no further need of Iceland.' This last suggestion was overstating the case, but within a decade vessels from Bristol were regularly fishing off Newfoundland, despite the long and risky voyage across the Atlantic. However, the fishery really took off later in the century. In 1578, fifty English vessels were said to be working there, 100 by 1592 and 250 by 1615. From the 1590s, some English vessels also began working further south, off the coast of what is now New England. Most of these came from the West Country, especially the ports of Devon, including Dartmouth, Plymouth, Appledore and Barnstaple. Fowey was the only Cornish port to take an active part in the trade.

This was a seasonal fishery. Large, square-rigged ships with crews of fifteen or twenty sailed in the early summer, taking up to a month to cross the Atlantic. Once they reached Newfoundland, crews set up their bases for the season – huts for accommodation, 'flakes' (racks) on which to dry the catch, and so on. The fish was dried in the sun and wind, and transported back across the Atlantic in 'sack' ships, ready for sale in southern Europe, where dried cod was a staple food. The fishing vessels themselves returned in the autumn. The Newfoundland fishery was an extraordinarily hard life for the crews. Newfoundland was a cold and inhospitable place, prone to long periods of heavy weather and dense fog. The fish were caught with hand-lines from small boats, dories, which in theory returned to shore each evening with their catches. Many, however, became lost in the fog or were overwhelmed and capsized in storms and disappeared without trace. From the second half of the seventeenth century, small sloops were used to work further offshore, on the Grand Banks themselves, which was no less dangerous.

Permanent settlement in New England began in the early seventeenth century, and fishing formed an important part of the economy of the early colonies, including, of course, that established by the Pilgrim Fathers in 1620. In Newfoundland, however, the harsh climate and lack of employment in the winter militated against permanent settlement. From the 1730s, however, people did begin to settle there in larger numbers, and the character of the fishery became steadily less migratory. The main catalyst was war, by which the Newfoundland fishery was always vulnerable to disruption. The transatlantic link was easily disrupted, export markets in southern Europe lost as powers such as Spain became hostile and, perhaps most importantly, men were pressed into the navy, whose need for manpower increased in every war between 1689 and 1815. The final, prolonged conflict with France after 1793 spelled the end of British involvement in the Newfoundland fishery, but by then a permanent population of around 20,000 had become established.

Another reason for the British withdrawal from the Newfoundland was that developments nearer home were making such a distant and risky business unnecessary. The white fisheries in the late eighteenth century, hitherto second to herring in importance, underwent a series of major developments that laid the foundations for their very rapid development in the nineteenth century. The road network was improving as turnpikes were established, which meant fish could be more quickly transported inland and arrive at market in better condition. Consequently, consumption began to rise, encouraged by the public authorities via measures such as an Act of Parliament of 1761 which exempted fish vans from post-horse dues and turnpike tolls on the roads into London. Transport was still slow and fish still had to be landed near to the point of sale, but the market had begun to widen.

Harwich, with its lining fleet, was already growing as a whitefish

Billingsgate Fish Market was established by Act of Parliament in 1699, and moved into a covered market hall in 1849. This lively scene was painted around 1808, when trading still took place in the open air.

port, but towards the end of the eighteenth century it began to face stiff competition from several places on the Thames estuary, especially Barking, Greenwich and Gravesend. These had the advantage of closer proximity to the London market, and had largely usurped the position of Harwich by 1800. Barking, now a part of east London's urban sprawl, was described by Scrymgeour Hewett as 'the prettiest village I ever did see' when he settled there in 1762. Hewett was already the owner of a fishing vessel, and his family firm, Hewett & Co, went on to become the largest and most successful of several family companies based at Barking. The firm's fleet was known as the 'Short Blue' fleet, because of the blue company flag they carried. Much of its success was based on line fishing on the Dogger Bank, and, as at Harwich, some fish were brought back alive in welled smacks and kept in cages in the Thames until market. Experiments were also made with trawling in the approaches to the Thames estuary and in the southern North Sea. Trawling, unlike lining, is an indiscriminate method of fishing that takes good and bad fish alike; but with the London market close at hand this mattered less than it did elsewhere, and the practice was well established in the Thames fishing fleets by 1815.

Trawling was also becoming established in Devon, especially around Tor Bay. Access to markets in Devon was always comparatively good because no major town in the county is more than thirty miles from a port, and with improvements to the roads it became possible to sell sufficient fish to make trawling worthwhile. Some Devon men also began working for the summer season off Kent, operating out of Dover and Ramsgate and selling their fish in London. In 1785, an estimated 100 small trawlers were operating from Brixham, the principal trawling port. They were landing fish worth more than £18,000, some of which was taken up country as far as Bath. The trawling smacks were small, single-masted vessels, less than forty tons, and since they were cheap to buy and operate many of them were owned outright by their skippers. These men could afford to save sufficient to put down a deposit with a ship-builder and take out a mortgage to cover the remainder from a local tradesman, perhaps a chandler or innkeeper, which was paid off over a period of years from the operating profits of the smack. This

Cornish fishing vessels of the seventeenth century, which probably closely resemble types used in earlier years. The crew of the vessel on the right appear to be hauling in a gill-net. (Mariner's Mirror 29 (1944))

also happened on the Thames, although here many more trawlers were owned by large family firms such as Hewett & Co or the firms owned by families such as the Morgans and Forges.

Another feature of the Barking and Devon fisheries was apprenticeship. This ancient institution, whereby boys lived with their masters and learned their trade in return for their keep becoming legally free at the age of twenty-one, was not wholly new to fishing. There are occasional references to apprenticed fishermen as far back as the sixteenth century, and famously George Crabbe's narrative poem *The Borough* of 1782 tells the tale of the cruel fisherman Peter Grimes, who murdered his apprentices. However, by 1800 apprenticeship was used much more widely than before. Most Brixham trawlers carried an apprentice, often the son of the skipper, or at least drawn from within the town and its surroundings, and the Barking companies recruited many pauper boys from the London workhouses. By 1850, Hewett & Co employed more than 200 apprentices. Paid only pocket money, if anything at all, apprentices were cheap to employ, and they learned skills that set them up to become skippers, and perhaps eventually owners, themselves. The single-ownership model and the apprenticeship system were to be vital to the trawl and line fisheries' future growth.

While the late eighteenth century was a time of innovation, expansion and dynamism in the fishing industry, as it was for the rest of the British economy, the great wars after 1793 caused great disruption and damage. Some fishermen were exempted from the press, but many were drawn into the navy, whilst such fishing as could go on was undertaken mainly by those too old, too young or too infirm for naval service. Trade routes were disrupted and export markets were lost, and fishing vessels were sometimes preyed upon by privateers. Britain emerged from the wars in 1815, however, in an exceptionally strong commercial position, and was to reap the benefits in coming years. Again, the fishing industry was to be no exception.

3.1 Parliamentary papers

During the eighteenth and, especially, the nineteenth centuries, governance in Britain became broader in scope and more effective.

Matters that previously would not have been attended to by government increasingly were, and the workings of government as a whole became more systematic. A growing volume of material was collected, processed, published and used as the basis for formulating policy. By the mid-nineteenth century the government was methodically enquiring into a great many areas of society and the economy, collecting and disseminating statistics and conducting detailed enquiries, the reports of which informed legislation. These changes related also to the fishing industry, and parliamentary papers on the subject form one of key groups of sources for anyone researching the industry and its workers.

Papers relating to fishing fall into three main categories. First, there are the texts of various Acts of Parliament. The preamble to these is often very interesting, as it sets out what the act was intended to achieve. However, the bulk of the text is made up of the detailed clauses of each act, in rather impenetrable legal language. These are likely to be the least useful parliamentary sources for most researchers.

Secondly, there are numerous statistical series. Some of these are one-offs, such as a return of accidental deaths aboard fishing vessels in 1880–2, but there are also regular series. From 1871, the Annual Statements of Navigation, which were the statistics detailing the numbers of ships and men at each port in Great Britain, include details of the number and type of fishing vessels and the approximate numbers needed to operate them. In 1886, the Fisheries Department of the Board of Trade was set up to monitor the industry. From the outset it published annual returns of the amount and species of fish landed in each port. These figures continue to the present day, although in a less detailed form, and all of them can be downloaded from the statistics section of the Marine and Fisheries Agency website (www.mfa.gov.uk/statistics/statistics.htm).

More usefully, the Fisheries Department also published an Annual Report of the Inspectors of Sea Fisheries. The first, in 1886, was a brief affair of only forty pages, but by the end of the century the reports had become much longer and far more detailed. They include a wealth of detail on the industry, ranging from scientific studies, returns of accidental deaths, conclusions of investigations into losses of fishing vessels and so on. From 1889 they also include a statement of the condition of the fisheries at every fishing port in the country, giving the types of fisheries conducted, the numbers of men and vessels employed, and matters affecting the fishing such as weather and market prices. These are obviously extremely useful for researching fishing at a given port, especially since even very small stations are included. However, individuals are very rarely identified, with the exception of local officials. Working fishermen are usually named only when they received gallantry awards, such as skipper Robert Page and third hand Charles Thurston of the Yarmouth smack *Problem*, who in 1897 were awarded a silver gallantry medal for rescuing the crew of the smack *Olive*, 'with considerable difficulty owing to a very heavy sea'. The outcomes of investigations into accidents are also listed, but here only the vessels involved are named and men are mentioned only by their ranks, although if you can find the vessel's crew list (see Chapter 4) for the time it is a simple matter to put names to the crew.

Thirdly, numerous parliamentary inquiries have been conducted into the fisheries since the eighteenth century. Some take a national view of the industry as a whole, others look at the fisheries of particular regions, and others still examine individual fisheries. Their published deliberations are among the most valuable sources available. They fall into three principal categories, which are still relevant now. Royal Commissions are appointed by the Crown to enquire into a particular issue, and although they often include politicians it is not essential that they do so. Select Committees are appointed by Parliament and are parliamentary bodies, all of whose members are MPs. Finally, departmental inquiries were generally composed of officials of the department concerned, MPs and experts, and had no obligation to publish their findings or the evidence presented to them, although many did.

Despite the technical differences between them, most of these inquiries were published in much the same format. Typically, there is at the beginning a minute setting out the aims and scope of the inquiry and any instructions given to the committee. This is followed by the report, and then the evidence. All inquiries involved interviewing witnesses, and full transcripts of their evidence are given. This is followed by appendices, which include written material given in by witnesses, relevant statistical material and sundry other items.

There are many exceptions, however. Some inquiries did not produce a report, for one reason or another, and published only the evidence presented to them. Conversely, departmental inquiries were not under obligation to publish evidence and frequently did not, leaving only a report. Generally, Royal Commissions produced the largest volume of material – the report and evidence of the Royal Commission on Sea Fisheries, published in 1866, occupies two large volumes – and departmental inquiries the least, some being only a few pages long. All of these are potentially very valuable, since they contain a wealth of detail on a wide variety of subjects connected with the fishing industry. Their reports are an invaluable source of contemporary perspective, they include statistical material that cannot be found elsewhere and they are almost the only place in

Landing fish in northern France in the 1950s. A typical scene, found at many small ports. (Basil Greenhill Collection)

which the words of vessel owners and some fishermen are recorded precisely as they were spoken.

To give one example, the most useful single document for those researching fishing labour in the nineteenth century is the Board of Trade inquiry into relations between owners, masters and men on fishing vessels, which was conducted in 1882, and whose conclusions informed the Merchant Shipping (Fishing Boats) Act of 1883. The report is a brief ten pages, but is followed by 162 pages of evidence, consisting of 6,465 questions asked of 129 witnesses at nine fishing ports and the Board of Trade offices in London. Finally, there are fifty-one appendices, including a full list of apprentices lost from Hull and Grimsby smacks in the previous few years, collected letters to newspapers alleging that boys were being 'decoyed' to Grimsby and apprenticed without their parents' knowledge, a previously unpublished report, lists of deserters from smacks at Great Yarmouth and a large amount of material on wages, numbers of vessels and suchlike.

There are, however, a few difficulties with parliamentary inquiries. Fishing vessel owners, especially leading figures, appear frequently and the changing opinions of some prominent individuals can be traced over time, but individual fishermen were asked to speak relatively rarely. Many witnesses naturally sought to portray themselves and their occupation in the best possible light, sometimes with the hope of influencing any legislation that might result, so much of the evidence can be decidedly self-serving. More practically, working through the pages of closely typed transcripts of evidence is a time-consuming job. Parliamentary inquiries are therefore not the first port of call for anyone seeking to trace an individual; but for anyone seeking to gain a deeper understanding of the industry they are very useful.

Access to parliamentary papers is comparatively easy. Only a limited amount is published in hard copy, but many university libraries hold a full set on microfiche, published by Chadwyck-Healey. Although accessing these can appear daunting, it is actually fairly simple. There are hard-copy indexes which are sorted by subject, so all of the inquiries mentioned above will be under 'fishing', with links to other relevant subject headings. Each paper is given, along with its year, volume number and page. For example, the 1882 inquiry is in the papers for that year, volume seventeen, pages 665–923, which when referenced will be rendered BPP [British Parliamentary Papers] 1882, XVII, 665–923. In addition, each fiche is numbered, and the numbers are also given in the Chadwyck-Healey indexes. On the fiches themselves, the handwritten number in the top right-hand corner of each double-page spread represents the page numbers given above.

As an alternative to using microfiches, a full set of parliamentary papers from 1801 to 2006 is now online on the Chadwyck-Healey website, at http://parlipapers.chadwyck.co.uk. However, this is a subscription service aimed at specialist libraries and educational institutions, which is not available to individuals. Using the site via a university library is therefore the best means of gaining access. Once you have managed to do so, it is fully searchable and all documents can be downloaded and printed as pdf files. Although printing or photocopying of parliamentary papers, especially of large documents such as inquiries, can be expensive, it is always useful to have hard copy.

The reports of several major inquiries were published by Her Majesty's Stationery Office, especially in the twentieth century, and can sometimes be found in hard copy, albeit usually only in academic libraries. Most of these are general reports on the state of the industry, such as the 1936 report of the Sea Fish Commission for the United Kingdom, an invaluable summary of the state of an industry which at the time was giving cause for concern. Some papers connected with this are in MAF 29 at the National Archives. Another example is the Committee of Inquiry into the Fishing Industry of 1961. In addition to the hard copy, forty-three files of papers connected with the enquiry are also at the National Archives, in class MAF 382.

3.2 Naval records

Naval records have been the subject of several books in their own right, so great is the volume of material. The best books on naval records for family historians are N A M Rodger's *Naval Records for Genealogists* (Public Record Office, 1998) and Bruno Pappalardo's *Tracing Your Naval Ancestors* (Public Record Office, 2002). A more detailed summary of the naval archives can be found in Randolph Cock and N A M Rodger's *A Guide to the Naval Records in the National Archives of the UK* (Institute of Historical Research, 2007). Few naval records tell you much about an individual's career before he joined the navy, but they contain a variety of interesting material on fishermen's naval service and some general material on fisheries.

Some fishermen served in the Sea Fencibles, a coastal defence force formed in 1798, when an invasion from France was a very real possibility. The Fencibles manned coastal defences and served in the revenue service, somewhat ironically, since many fishermen had some involvement in smuggling. The attraction of serving with them was immunity from militia service and the press gang. They were disbanded in 1810, when the invasion threat had subsided. Sea Fencibles pay books can be found in ADM 28, arranged by region.

One place where individuals outside the navy in the eighteenth century can be found is the registers of protections. Exemptions from impressment, known as protections, were granted to seamen engaged in important work. If a man was taken up by the press gang and could show a protection he had to be sent back, although there were occasions when desperate need for men caused the navy to send out a 'hot press', which ignored protections. There are several registers of protections in the National Archives, all in class ADM 7. It is difficult to tell which ones include fishermen, but ADM 7/381–6 and ADM 7/388 certainly do. They cover wartime periods between 1755 and 1815. Unfortunately, names are not indexed, so searching through them can be a slightly laborious job, although they are fairly legible.

Generally, the information given becomes clearer and more full over time, but in most cases the name of man and ship are given, along with a port and sometimes – more often later – a note on the trade the man was engaged in. For men in merchant ships this is usually rendered as a trade such as 'coastal' or 'coal trade', or perhaps a trading destination – 'Baltick', 'Dantzick' (Danzig) and so on. Fishermen are often not marked in the early registers, but later ones frequently include an explanation such as 'mackerel fishery' or 'cod fishing', from which you can deduce roughly what fishery an individual was working in, and sometimes a home port. Some scattered records, mainly letters, relating to impressment also

Name	Master			Port	Remarks
Eliza	R. Roe	87	4 2	Meall	Brick & Coasting
Enterprize	J. Crockley	81	5	Barton	"
Milford	J. Phillips	40	2 1	Milford	
Nanny	W. Roberts	110	4 3	Swanzea	Coal & Coasting
Speculator	W. Stephenson	120	7	Sunderld	Ballast
Hope	W. Palmer	148	6 2	Harbro	Employed in bringing Tea from Holland for the Service of the E. I. Compy
Betsey	J. Fleck	300	10 3	"	"
Unity	J. Osmond	140	8 2	Shields	"
Sally	Ja Totham	51	4 3	Harwich	Fishing
Ja & Ann	Ja Reason	40	"	"	"
Peggy & Patty	J. Bacon	54	"	"	"
Owners Consent	J. Kewley	50	"	"	"
Robt & Sarah	J. South	52	"	"	"
Robt & Mary	J. Clark	50	"	"	"
Geo & Mary	J. Shuffel	45	"	"	"
New Providence	J. Cooper	56	"	"	"
Susanna	Ja Keeble	45	"	"	"
Friend Goodwill	J. Pain	40	"	"	"
Elizabeth	S. Hall	50	"	"	"
Amity	J. Rainbird	40	"	"	"
Polly	Rd Wood	54	"	"	"
William	J. Dunnet	55	1	"	"
Brokers Adventure	Adventure	52	"	"	"
Good Intent	W. Saunders	50	4	"	"
Providence	S. Ketleby	56	"	"	"
John & Ruth	J. Burton	52	"	"	"
John & Rebecca	W. McDonough	"	"	"	"
John & Grace	Ja Lark	45	"	"	"
Jno & Elizabeth	Jno Seymour	52	"	"	"
Polly	D. Gregson	"	"	"	"

survive in local archives. There is also sundry other material in ADM 7, such as returns of men raised for the navy, which may include names of those who were pressed.

Impressment was phased out during the nineteenth century when, instead, the Royal Naval Reserve was established to provide a pool of manpower for the navy to draw on in wartime. Fishermen were largely overlooked until 1911, when the Trawler section of the reserve was established. Trawlers were to be hired at an agreed rate from owners participating in the scheme, and crews who were members of the Reserve were to serve aboard them. Hiring soon gave way to requisitioning of both trawlers and drifters, and vessels were requisitioned again as another war loomed in 1939. Thus many fishing vessels and fishermen saw service in both world wars, and some records covering both can be found. Many of them are closely related to the normal crew records kept in peacetime and are discussed in the next chapter. However, there are some useful documents elsewhere in the archives.

The letters of the Admiral Commanding Reserves are in Class ADM 120 at the National Archives, and will include material on the Trawler Reserve. Class ADM 137 contains a miscellany of material collected by the Admiralty's Historical Section for its official history of the navy in the First World War, including some records on the service and loss of trawlers on war service. Most pieces in this series are described in the catalogue only by a document number, an index to which is contained in ADM 12. A few pieces likely to be of particular interest are ADM 137/2653, which includes the monthly reports of the Anti-Submarine Division between June 1817 and October 1918, ADM 137/1931, containing notes on Special Service vessels, including trawlers, and ADM 137/1213, on decoy vessels. Other documents of interest are the records of stations during the First World War, especially of Plymouth in ADM 131, which contains various papers on the operation of the Auxiliary Patrol, which included many fishing vessels. ADM 156 contains the records

Opposite page: *A page of the register of exemptions from impressment, 1793–1801. Note that fishermen are marked in the right-hand column. (The National Archives, ADM7/385)*

of courts martial, roughly sorted by date and including some cases arising from the reserves, among them fishermen.

Regarding individuals, only a 'representative sample' of reservists' service records has been preserved, in BT 164. These are sorted by individuals' service numbers, to which an index is contained in BT 377/7–28. The index shows the full name, age, place of birth and service number of all reservists except those whose service numbers began with the code SBC, the index for which has not survived. Unfortunately, there is nothing in the indexes to show whose records have been preserved, so all you can do is find the individual's service number and then order the relevant part of BT 164 in the hope that his records will be there.

The skippers of armed fishing vessels appear on the Navy List, the confidential edition of which used during the wars can be found on shelves in the reading room, classed ADM 177. There is no separate index of Trawler Reserve men, but they appear in the main alphabetical list of reserve officers, and some editions also have a list of auxiliary vessels, which also gives the skipper's name. Some officers' records may also exist in ADM 240. Some ships' logs for both world wars can be found in ADM 53, sorted by ships' names and by year. However, not all logs survive and for fishing vessels there are evidently few beyond 1940.

Some fishermen were unfortunate enough to end up as prisoners of war. For the First World War no comprehensive indexes of prisoners survive, but lists of merchant seamen and fishermen detained in Germany, Austria-Hungary and Turkey do exist, dated 21 September 1915 (FO 383/65, file 67310, paper 146257), 31 March 1917 (FO 383/352, file 4651, paper 92439), 31 July 1917 (CO 693/5, file 45094, folios 509–567) and 31 December 1917 (CO 693/9, file 3957, folios 454–503), and some may appear in the card index to prisoners whose names appear in the Foreign Office's General Correspondence (FO 371). For the Second World War the records are more comprehensive and can be found in the Merchant Seamen Prisoner of War Records in BT 373, arranged by ship and by name. These include details such as name, rating, prisoner of war number, date and place of birth, date of loss of ship and next of kin.

Those who were killed on active service between 1939 and 1945 are recorded on a Roll of Honour, which can be found at BT 339/8, arranged according to name. Unfortunately, no similar list exists for the First World War, although the Commonwealth War Graves Commission Debt of Honour register includes names of civilians lost at sea and details of where they are commemorated. The register is searchable by name, from a link on the Commonwealth War Graves Commission homepage, www.cwgc.org.

The Royal Navy protected British fishing vessels working off Iceland during the disputes known as the Cod War, and some records of this service in 1971–3 can be found in FCO 33/1313 and 2026–30. Some sound recordings of radio communication between Icelandic and British naval vessels and fishing boats are in the National Sound Archive, reference G31/01/01–07.

Anything more recent than this is likely still to be under official closure.

3.3 Records of the Newfoundland fishery

Newfoundland was England's first overseas colony. It was founded in 1583, and from an early date the government took a keen interest in its economy, of which fishing was the most important part. Accordingly, the papers of the Colonial Office and its predecessor bodies contain a wealth of material on the Newfoundland fishery.

At the National Archives, class CO 1 contains the colonial series of papers generated by the Privy Council from 1574 to 1757. This includes Replies to Heads of Enquiry, which constitute a form of census of the colony and the fisheries. Most of these date from the 1670s to 1690s, and are effectively head counts of the resident planters and visiting ships at various settlements during the summer fishing season, taken by naval officers. Most include at least the names of ships and usually their captains as well, as well as a return of the number of boats and men. Some also give numbers of wives and children resident at the time.

From 1696, records of the fishery continue in class CO 194. The annual Returns of Fisheries are more statistical than the previous surveys, consisting of figures on the numbers of boats and men working, fish caught, processing facilities used and so on. CO 194 also contains a wealth of correspondence on various matters, mostly government business but also including some matters related to the fishery. In war years throughout the eighteenth century, for instance, there are numerous petitions from merchants in the British ports sending ships to the fishery complaining of the hardship caused by enemy action and the press gang. Records in both CO 1 and CO 194 are ordered by year.

From an early date the Royal Navy stationed ships at Newfoundland to protect the fishery, and from 1729 to 1824 the Commander-in-Chief on the station was also the governor of the colony. As a result, some records of the fishery can be found in the Admiralty archives. An account of the colony and fisheries of Newfoundland dating from 1677 is in ADM 7/689, whilst a survey of the fisheries from 1774 can be found in ADM 1/5117/4. The correspondence of successive Commanders-in-Chief on the station, also in ADM 1, may possibly yield some information as well, although it will be buried amid a mass of detail on naval matters and some of it may well duplicate letters in CO 194. The correspondence of admirals on other stations where fishing vessels would often be encountered might contain some discussion of fishing, generally in terms of protecting fishermen from enemy activity, but this is definitely a long shot and any information will certainly be very general.

A considerable amount of material relating to the Newfoundland fishery can also be found in the archives at the Rooms, in St John's Newfoundland. Further information can be found on their website at www.therooms.ca.

Further Reading

Hervey Benham, *The Codbangers* (Essex County Newspapers, 1979)
John Dyson, *Business in Great Waters* (Angus and Robertson, 1977)
D J Starkey, C Reid and N Ashcroft, *England's Sea Fisheries: The Commercial Sea Fisheries of England and Wales since 1300* (Chatham, 2000)

Chapter Four

THE TRAWL AND LINE FISHERIES, 1815–1950

When peace returned in 1815, recovery was sometimes slow, especially in the south. A Select Committee report from 1833 remarked on the 'great decay and distress' of the fishery at Harwich, and matters were little better across much of the south coast, although further north the situation was generally better. Nevertheless, the three decades after 1815 witnessed developments that laid the foundations for the expansion and transformation of the industry in subsequent years.

The trawl fishery based in Devon was quickly back on its feet after 1815, and by the 1820s Brixham and Plymouth trawling smacks had resumed their seasonal working off Kent and in the southern North Sea. From around 1830, some began to settle permanently at Ramsgate, which gradually emerged as a leading trawling port. Some experimental trawling was also conducted further north, off the Yorkshire coast, in 1819 and 1821. This was not an immediate success because the men were unfamiliar with the grounds and suffered damage to their gear, but the area clearly had potential. Ten years later, Devon and Ramsgate trawlers returned and began to work from Scarborough, by then a fashionable summer resort for the wealthy where fresh fish fetched good prices. During the 1830s a small number began to settle there permanently, and later in the decade some also settled at the larger town of Hull.

It was in the line and trawl fisheries based in the Thames estuary, however, that innovations key to the future of the fishery were being introduced. The largest firm, Hewett & Co of Barking, pioneered the practice of 'fleeting,' sending trawlers to sea in fleets for up to eight weeks at a time and servicing them daily with a fast cutter that took out supplies and brought the fish to market. Fleeting increased the amount of time each smack spent fishing and was therefore more efficient, although spending eight weeks at a stretch at sea in all weathers, aboard small vessels with one cabin and no sanitary facilities was a hard life for the crews. Hewett & Co are also credited with pioneering the use of ice to keep the fish cool at sea. Between them, ice and fleeting ensured a more regular supply of fish to market, which arrived in better condition and fetched higher prices. Needless to say, both innovations were soon adopted elsewhere.

Commercial fishing was still limited by the age-old problem of transport. Unless it was to be cured, fish had to be landed near to market, or it arrived in too decayed a condition to be saleable. This largely restricted fishermen to a local market, and limited the possibility of supplying fresh fish to towns and cities inland. The

A fleet at sea. Trawlers fished in fleets of up to 100, staying at sea for eight weeks at a time.

railways, faster and cheaper than road transport, finally broke this bottleneck. Small amounts of prime fish were taken to market by rail from about 1840, but early railway companies were more interested in taking over passenger traffic and bulk goods from the roads than developing new freight flows, and it was the mid-1850s before carriage rates were lowered far enough for large amounts of cheaper fish to find their way inland. By this time, however, several railway companies had spotted the potential of fish traffic, and their involvement transformed the fishing industry. At Grimsby, then a small and isolated town, the Manchester, Sheffield and Lincolnshire Railway sank £7,000 into building the first dedicated fish dock, which opened in 1857, and followed this up by paying bounties and building houses to entice fishermen to the port. This was the trigger for a spectacular boom that within thirty years made Grimsby into the largest whitefish port in the country.

The MS&LR's decision to develop Grimsby as a port was influenced by another development of the early 1840s, the opening up of productive new trawling grounds around the Dogger Bank. These had long been worked by local line fishermen, but sometime around 1840 they were 'discovered' by Devon trawlers. Reputedly, these visitors were blown off course in a winter storm, and when they were able to recover their nets found them full of high-quality soles; so full, according to some versions of the tale, that the nets were torn away from the beams altogether. The reality may have been more mundane, but in cold winters the valuable catches from these grounds were real enough, and they were another spur to the burgeoning offshore trawl fisheries of the North Sea. They helped to attract more migrants to the Humber ports, and also to Lowestoft, where Devon and Kent men began to settle around 1860.

More migrants came from the Thames, whose fisheries began to decline as the railways made it quicker and cheaper to land fish in East Anglia and transport it to London by rail than to sail up to Billingsgate. The trade in live, line-caught cod was also damaged by the worsening pollution of the Thames, which made it impossible to keep fish alive. Hewett & Co moved their fleet wholesale from Barking to Great Yarmouth in 1854, followed soon afterwards by others. Harwich also experienced a revival as a base for long-liners.

Migrant trawlers were not always welcomed. In Hull the Dock

Company regarded them as a nuisance and until the late 1860s failed to provide sufficient facilities for them, leading some to move to Grimsby as that port became better established. Elsewhere, visitors were greeted with outright hostility. A visiting trawlerman was stabbed at Scarborough in 1832, and there were periodic scuffles at several ports. Trawlers often damaged the gear of local line fishermen, and their large catches could glut markets and depress prices. They were also accused of destroying fish stocks, and the suggestion was made that migration northwards was caused by exhaustion of the grounds further south. This last was not true, but so serious was the controversy that a Royal Commission on Sea Fisheries was set up in 1863. Its report, published in 1866, was

Manning the capstan to haul in drift nets aboard a North Sea lugger.
Later, this task was made easier with the introduction of steam capstans.
(Mariner's Mirror *19 (1933)*

crucial to the future of the industry. It argued that no proof existed of overfishing and, in line with the laissez-faire philosophy of the day, recommended that existing regulations be repealed and 'unrestricted freedom of fishing be permitted hereafter.' Trawling had the official green light to continue.

Between 1840 and 1880, the trawl and line fisheries all around the country grew at an unprecedented rate. There were fewer than fifty trawlers on the Humber in the mid-1840s; forty years later Hull and Grimsby had over 1,000 between them, and at most other ports, even those such as Brixham which experienced substantial outward migration, the numbers and size of trawlers grew. Early smacks were single-masted vessels of less than forty tons; by the late 1870s, those built for the Humber ports and Great Yarmouth were two-masted, ketch-rigged vessels of eighty tons and more, fitted with steam-powered capstans to assist with hauling the new and heavier trawls. Those used at other ports were usually smaller, although steam capstans and ketch, or 'dandy,' rig were introduced there too. Along with rising numbers of boats, ancillary industries such as insurance, net-making, shipbuilding and fish sales and processing were established, often owned by consortia of smack-owners. The leading figures in the industry, especially on the Humber, became wealthy and influential men. Most magistrates at Grimsby had some involvement in fishing, and in Hull smack-owner Henry Toozes became Mayor in 1887. Former outsiders were now civic dignitaries.

There was one potential obstacle for the industry to overcome. Fishing had become established in places with no tradition of fishing and no pool of skilled labour to draw on. The solution lay with an expansion of the apprenticeship system that was familiar to owners from both the Thames and Devon, and through which many of them had started their careers. Apprenticeship was thought to make good fishermen, but owners were also well aware that apprentices were cheap to employ and their indentures banned them from striking or absenting themselves from work. Cheap labour was needed, and in the fast-growing ports of the Humber hundreds of teenagers were brought in each year to provide it. By 1878, apprentices outnumbered paid hands at Grimsby by 1,790 to 1,680, and the situation was similar in Hull. Fewer apprentices were

Ramsgate smacks, making their way slowly out of harbour in light winds, around 1900.

employed in East Anglia, where casual labour was easier to find, and in Brixham and Ramsgate apprentices made up about a quarter of the workforce. Even so, there were more than 4,000 apprentices in the fishing industry nationally by the mid-1870s.

At ports such as Brixham, apprentices were usually recruited from within the community and were often related to fishermen, as had long been the case. They were indentured around the age of fourteen, although sometimes younger, and 'came out of their time,' as it was known, when they were twenty-one. They began as cooks and were promoted to deckhands for the last few years of their term. During that time, they were paid only pocket money and lived with their masters, or in lodgings he found for them. This paternalistic system worked reasonably well, but on the Humber it changed for the worse from the late 1850s.

Many apprentices were recruited from workhouses or reformatories, or were waifs and strays from the cities, and some certainly signed their indentures with no real idea of what they were committing themselves to. Moreover, wealthy owners with fleets of smacks and dozens of apprentices had neither space nor inclination to keep them at home, and instead began paying their apprentices a living allowance and leaving them to fend for themselves, a practice known as the 'outdoor' system. Unsupervised, many drifted into the slums of the Victorian port towns, lodging in cheap boarding houses, pubs and brothels. 'Quite small boys,' commented a report on the condition of apprentices at Grimsby from 1872, 'told me they could without difficulty get served with as much beer as they wanted.' Predictably enough, drunkenness, prostitution and brawling became all too common. Smack-owners took little interest in their apprentices' welfare as long as they turned up for work when required. If they did not, or if they attempted to run away, they could be taken to court and, if they refused to return to work, sentenced to three months' hard labour, sometimes by a magistrate who was himself a smack-owner. About a quarter of Hull and Grimsby apprentices absconded. Many more tried, but were arrested and brought back, and some ran away repeatedly in the hope that masters would lose patience and cancel their indentures. Such was the need for labour, however, that owners were usually reluctant to let even the most recalcitrant apprentices leave. Some served multiple terms in prison for absconding, and yet still completed their apprenticeships.

Trawling was a hard and dangerous occupation. Those in the crew who were not apprentices were usually paid by a share of the profits of each trip. The work of hauling the trawl and dealing with the catch was exhausting, and went on constantly when the catches were good. Accidents were commonplace as men worked with unguarded machinery on slippery decks in all weathers. Living conditions aboard the smacks were primitive, with one cabin shared by all of the crew. The shares system, although it paid well when catches were valuable, put everyone under pressure to work as hard as possible, except when the weather was either too rough or too calm to fish, at which point no- one was earning any money and boredom and frustration inevitably set in. In these conditions, some

crews lost patience with resentful, frightened or clumsy apprentices. Bullying, 'petty tyranny and horseplay of a rough nature' as
one report described it, was common; serious violence and sexual
assaults not unknown.

The apprenticeship system slipped into decline from the 1870s.
Settlement over the previous few decades had created working-
class fishing communities around the fishing ports, such as the
Hessle Road in Hull, from where recruits could be drawn.
Elsewhere the agricultural depression of the 1870s pushed workers
off the land and made casual labour cheaper, which virtually killed
off apprenticeship in the East Anglian ports. Meanwhile, a change
in the law in 1880 removed masters' power of summary detention
and allowed apprentices to desert in large numbers. Smack-owners
argued vigorously for the law to return to its old state, but the
government was against this and popular pressure for action
followed when in July 1882 the story emerged of how Hull skipper
Osmond Brand had subjected fourteen-year-old apprentice William
Papper to a fortnight of starvation and gross physical abuse. Papper
had died as a result, and Brand threw the body overboard and
reported the death as an accident. This was accepted until another
member of the crew went to the police and told the full story. Brand
was hanged for murder, as was the mate of another Hull smack,
Edward Wheatfield, convicted of killing apprentice Peter Hughes a
couple of months later. Legislation was now inevitable, and the
more enlightened owners co-operated with the Merchant Shipping
(Fishing Boats) Act of 1883, which banned the outdoor system,
appointed superintendents to oversee the apprenticeship system
and introduced a raft of measures to regulate the industry better,
such as crew lists and mandatory certificates of competency for
skippers.

The decline of apprenticeship was one facet of wider changes in
the relationship between owners and crews. The cost of smacks was
rising and profits dwindling as the fears of early opponents of
trawling began to be realised and the North Sea began to show signs
of overfishing. It had become far more difficult for working
fishermen to purchase their own vessels, and the industry in many
places was becoming concentrated in the hands of a small number
of powerful trawler owners. This became increasingly obvious as

fleeting was introduced on the Humber in the 1870s, and then enforced all year round, using steam cutters owned by consortia of leading smack-owners to service the fleets.

Fleeting was more efficient and more profitable than operating trawlers singly, but for crews it represented much longer periods of hard work and worsening conditions. Fresh food supplies were limited, living conditions became harsher as there was no opportunity to clean the cabins or for men to wash, and the dangers increased. Dozens of smacks working close together in all weathers were at risk of collisions, and transferring the fish from smack to cutter by open boat was fraught with danger. There were no medical facilities, so injured men had to be ferried home on the cutter for treatment. In calm weather, cheap spirits obtained from 'coper' vessels plying among the fleets led to drunken accidents and occasional violence. To combat the copers, the Mission to Deep Sea Fishermen, founded in 1881, fitted out a number of smacks of its own. These served as hospital ships, and also distributed religious literature and useful goods such as warm clothing donated by the Mission's supporters.

Fishing had little tradition of trade unionism, but discontent spread among large numbers of men working for a few powerful employers, and in the 1880s there were periodic strikes at Hull, Grimsby and Great Yarmouth. The largest was sparked off by the Great Gale of 3–6 March 1883, which devastated the fleets working on the Dogger Bank. As many as 350 men may have died. The resulting strike did secure some restrictions on the operation of fleets in winter, but fleeting continued because it was often the only way to make sailing trawlers profitable.

The way out of the impasse lay with steam power. A few converted paddle-steamers had been working inshore since 1877, and the first purpose-built steam trawlers were introduced in 1882. They were very successful, and they offered the possibility of working outside the North Sea. In 1891, Icelandic grounds were trawled for the first time, and later the Bay of Biscay and the Barents Sea were explored. These early distant-water ventures were risky, working right at the edge of trawlers' range, but larger and faster vessels were soon constructed, and the fishing effort of Hull and Grimsby and newly established ports such as Aberdeen, Milford

Haven and Fleetwood switched increasingly to distant waters. The North Sea was still fished, but the fleets were in terminal decline. The Great Yarmouth fleets were sold off in the 1890s and trawling from the port virtually ceased. Lowestoft, Ramsgate and the ports of the south-west retained their sailing smacks, which could still make a profit from catching smaller quantities of high-quality fish. Hull was the only port to persist with fleeting, keeping a fleet of small steam trawlers operating in the North Sea until 1936.

Steam trawling revolutionized the business of fishing, necessitating the formation of companies to finance the building of trawlers and organise the operations needed to maintain and supply them. Several leading smack-owners converted their businesses into limited companies during the 1890s. For the men, steam trawlers were safer and more comfortable than the smacks, although living quarters were still very basic. Crews doubled in size, and a division emerged between deck and engine room hands that sometimes caused friction which owners were quick to exploit when necessary. A major dispute blew up at Grimsby in 1901 over changes to the system of payment by shares, which caused the well-organized engineers to strike, followed shortly afterwards by skippers and deck crews. The dispute dragged on for fourteen weeks. Initially it was peaceful, but violence broke out after one owner attempted to man his trawlers with foreign crews, and the offices of the trawler owners' federation were ransacked and burned down. The Riot Act was read, and troops called in to restore order. Eventually, the dispute was taken to arbitration and a compromise was reached. The Grimsby dispute marked an end to effective trade unionism among fishermen, since skippers, deck crews and engineers were represented by different organizations and owners were able to play them off against one another, a pattern repeated in subsequent disputes.

In 1913, the British fishing industry as a whole landed more than 800,000 tons of fish, caught by a fleet of nearly 9,500 boats, including 1,200 trawlers, which employed more than 37,000 men at sea and tens of thousands more in related industries ashore. The line fishery had faded out, and by 1900 was concentrated almost entirely at Grimsby. The trawl fishery in many ways had assumed the form it would keep for half a century: changes in vessel design, labour

Smacksmen rowing fish to the steam cutter, mid-1880s. So dangerous was this job in winter that men are said to have refused promotion to avoid it.

regime, marketing arrangements and business organization were to be changes in degree rather than in kind.

The First World War seriously disrupted the industry. Already the potential of trawlers for minesweeping had been spotted, and many were hired in the run-up to war, although the numbers were insufficient and hiring soon gave way to requisitioning. The arrangements for reserving crews for them were inadequate, however, and many fishermen had enlisted in the army where their skills were largely wasted. For those who did serve in the Royal Naval Trawler Reserve there were the tasks of minesweeping and anti-submarine operations, and the necessity of getting used to naval discipline. Relationships between officers and men on a trawler – insofar as the distinction even existed – were in stark contrast to the formality of the navy, and naval officers at times despaired of fishermen who smoked, spat in the water and waved to friends on the quayside when supposed to be standing to attention. An official blind eye was usually turned to minor lapses of discipline, however, because there was no denying that the fishermen were doing an exceptionally dangerous and demanding job, and doing it well. Armed fishing vessels proved to be very effective minesweepers, towing devices which cut through mines' anchoring lines and forced them to the surface where they could be detonated by gunfire. Needless to say this was extremely dangerous, and many trawlers were lost to the mines they were trying to destroy. Trawlers also operated as armed patrol craft. They scored several confirmed submarine kills, but perhaps more importantly their very presence forced U-boats to remain submerged for longer periods of time. This blunted the effectiveness of the U-boats and must have saved many merchant ships from destruction.

For those who remained fishing, mainly those too old or young for the forces, the normal dangers of fishing were exacerbated by enemy action. Many fishing vessels were attacked by surface raiders and submarines, and 673 were lost. The ports of western Britain experienced a resurgence as fishing effort in the North Sea was cut back, and for a while obsolete sailing trawlers again made a major contribution to landings. Some vessels that did continue to fish were fitted with concealed guns and sent out as 'Q-ships.' U-boats did not generally reckon it worthwhile to torpedo fishing vessels and instead ordered their crews to abandon ship and sank them with gunfire or bombs placed aboard. Therefore, if U-boats could be induced to come close enough, guns could be used to destroy them before they had a chance to submerge again. Even a few sailing trawlers were thus fitted, and succeeded in sinking several U-boats. Famously, skipper Tom Crisp of Lowestoft was awarded a posthumous Victoria Cross for an attempt to fight off a U-boat with the smack *I'll Try*. Ashore, the supply of fish inevitably fell and prices rocketed, leading to some resentment against those who did continue fishing and made healthy profits as a result.

After the Armistice in 1918, the priority of the industry was to get back to normal as soon as possible, once the complex task of demobilising ships and men was completed. 'Normality' was taken to mean the conditions prevailing in 1913, but this was never to happen. After a brief boom in 1919–21, prices slumped, fishing grounds untouched during the war began to show signs of exhaustion again and uncharted wrecks caused expensive gear losses. Many were caught in a vicious circle of rising costs, declining catches and low profits, and structural faults that had mattered little in the good years before 1914 now plagued the industry. Fundamentally, there were too many and too small players, lacking capital to invest in their parts of the industry and making reforms difficult to agree upon and put into effect. The result was stagnation in many places, especially those whose fishing boats were mainly deployed in the North Sea. Few new trawlers were built for Aberdeen or Grimsby, so the fleet grew older, less efficient and less profitable, and for crews they offered dismal living and working conditions, and low earnings. Many were still coal-fired, even though oil, which new trawlers used from the 1930s, was cleaner, and easier and cheaper to handle.

As in many other trades, earnings fell during the 1920s and there were occasional strikes, some of them bitter but none of them successful, although a strike in Hull in 1935 did lead to the formation of a fishermen's section of the Transport and General Workers' Union. The attitude of the owners, however, remained as intransigent as ever. Smaller ports usually struggled, and sometimes went into terminal decline. The small Boston trawling fleet transferred to Grimsby in the 1920s and the Ramsgate fleet never recovered from the war. Sailing trawlers continued to work from Lowestoft and Brixham and a few were built new until 1926, but their numbers dwindled, until the last few in service at the Suffolk port were towed up to Lake Lothing in 1939 and used as a barrage against invasion craft.

In contrast to the stagnation evident in many ports, Hull presented 'an air of enterprise and confidence,' and was a conspicuous success between the wars. In Hull there were fewer but larger trawler firms who were better able to co-operate in changing the industry and keeping it profitable. After 1936, Hull was exclusively a distant-water port, and it built newer, larger and more efficient trawlers to exploit new grounds north of the Arctic Circle such as Bear Island and Spitsbergen. The fish landed from here was coarser than that from further south, but ideal for the fish and chip trade, which absorbed between a third and a half of whitefish landings at the time. Minimum sale prices were fixed to prevent market crashes, and more fish was filleted before being sent inland, the resulting offal being processed profitably into fish meal at a plant owned jointly by the trawler firms. Hull doubled its share of whitefish landings to 45 per cent by 1937.

The Second World War had much the same effect on the industry as the previous war. The North Sea was expected again to become too dangerous for fishing, and trawlers which were to continue working were reassigned to west coast ports less likely to be affected by enemy action. Hull, soon to become one of the most bomb-damaged cities in the country, ceased to function as a fishing port altogether, and other ports on the east coast fared little better. More than 800 trawlers, mainly the largest and newest, were bought or requisitioned for minesweeping and patrol duties. The Admiralty also built trawlers of its own which were sold cheaply to owners after the war as partial compensation for their losses. This time, however, the manning of Reserve trawlers was better managed. Fishermen were placed on the list of Reserved Occupations and called up for service as required. This worked well on the whole, although the old cultural differences and friction between naval officers and trawlermen soon re-emerged. Armed trawlers again undertook convoy escort, minesweeping and patrolling duties, and around 260 were lost by enemy action and accidents.

For those who continued to fish, the threat of attack from the air was added to the hazards of the previous war. The first trawler was lost off Tory Island sixteen days after war was declared, and thereafter fishermen were regularly subjected to air and submarine attack. Eighty-eight steam trawlers and 827 men were lost to enemy action in addition to many other fishing vessels, mainly in the first two years of the war. Ashore, fish was never rationed but price controls had to be introduced in 1941 as falling landings sent prices soaring.

At the end of the war there was again a brief boom. The grounds had been rested for six years so catches were large and prices were high. Those who were demobilised and able to fish in the immediate post-war years made good money, but prices collapsed in 1949 as markets became glutted, and even before this the trade's long-standing problems of obsolete ships, overfishing and low investment had started to show again. The near- and middle-water sectors, those fishing mainly around the North and Irish Seas and the Faroe Islands and the eastern Atlantic, were worst affected, and in response the Labour government set up the White Fish Authority to oversee a programme of grants, loans and subsidies designed to help the industry reform, which had some success. At this stage the distant-water sector was profitable, and so was not included in the scheme until a few years later.

The trawl fishery of the 1950s has been described as 'antiquated,' and in some respects it had changed little in fifty years. Vessels were of the same basic design as those of 1900, albeit larger and faster, and diesel engines were slowly replacing steam. They were working principally the same grounds as before the war, to supply a distribution network that was fundamentally unchanged from the form it had assumed in the nineteenth century. They were owned by limited-liability firms, often directly descended from those formed in the transition to steam trawling half a century before. These firms were in a powerful position vis-à-vis their crews, since by this time there was a surplus of labour and owners could pick and choose men, who were technically casual labour and had few rights. A skipper who caught too little or an unpopular deckhand could be sacked on the spot, and men regarded as troublesome could be blacklisted and left unable to find work. Persistent rumours were aired of men offering bribes to get on the best ships. Trawler owners naturally denied this, but there was no doubt that it went on.

Fishermen were drawn from working-class areas around the docks. Boys went to sea at fifteen or sixteen as cook's mates or deckie-learners. Those that stuck at it were made deckhands, and then depending on ability bosuns, mates and potentially skippers, although few made it that far. Engineers trained ashore before joining trawlers, and wireless operators were not employed by trawler firms at all, but by the Marconi company. The system of payment had changed little: skippers were paid entirely by a share of the profits, everyone else a small basic wage and 'poundage,' a percentage of the profits dependent on rank. If a voyage failed to cover expenses, the crew got nothing above their basic wage, and could in fact technically end up in debt to the company.

A distant-water fishing trip lasted about three weeks, ten days of which were spent actually fishing. Once on the grounds, fishing went on constantly unless the weather was too bad, and no sooner was the trawl hauled and emptied than it was shot away again and the deckhands could turn their hand to gutting and icing the fish heaped on deck. Not until 1947 were there any rules on working hours, and then men were entitled to six hours off in twenty-four, unless some emergency demanded their continuing to work. The trawlerman of the 1950s worked an average week of ninety hours.

It was a hard job, and it was dangerous. Tired men working unguarded winches on icy decks in bad weather inevitably had accidents, skippers fishing close to the shore sometimes misjudged their position and ran aground, and the constant pressure on skippers to make large catches meant that some continued to fish in bad weather, beyond the margin of safety. For those working in the far north, there was the added danger of 'icing up,' as spray froze all over the trawler and gave her a potentially lethal coating of ice. In 1955 the Hull trawler *Kingston Garnet* fouled her propeller off north-west Iceland. *Lorella* and *Roderigo*, also Hull trawlers, set out to assist, but within hours they were badly iced up and sending out frantic distress signals. *Kingston Garnet* managed to free her propeller and limp to safety, but *Lorella* and *Roderigo* had both capsized before help could reach them, and in the intense cold there was no hope of rescue for the forty men aboard.

Fishermen were renowned for their fatalism, and accidents were seen as part of the job. Although many came to wish they had gone into a more secure and less taxing job, the relatively good wages and the lifestyle kept many at it until injury or declining fitness forced them to retire. Fishermen were known ashore as 'three-day millionaires,' since with sixty hours in dock between trips many took the opportunity to spend most of the time in the pubs and clubs. Many missed a trip or two a year, during which they could claim unemployment benefit, but there was no sick pay, no pension and no job security.

The trawl fishery of the 1950s was a direct descendant of that which had taken shape towards the end of the nineteenth century, when the technology of fishing, many of the main grounds, the marketing systems and the communities in which the men lived had taken shape. However, as the last chapter explores, fundamental and painful changes lay close in the future.

4.1 Crew lists and agreements

Crew lists and agreements had existed for merchant ships in one form or another since 1786, but most of the fishing industry was not covered. Fishing boats registered under the Merchant Shipping Act of 1854 (see Chapter 5) were supposed to make out crew lists, but not all did.

The breakdown of the apprenticeship system as well as widespread desertion and wage disputes led to fishing vessel crew lists being introduced under the Fishing Boats Act of 1883. However, this was not a simple matter. The fishing industry varied widely from place to place, many vessels made only short voyages that made the drawing up of crew lists for each impractical, and in any case the abuses that the 1883 Act aimed to correct arose mainly aboard larger trawlers. Consequently, the rules were framed only to apply to certain sectors, although they were gradually extended over time.

From 1 January 1884, skippers or owners of fishing vessels of greater than twenty-five tons were obliged to enter into written agreements with their crews, on the official Crew List and Agreement form. The twenty-five ton minimum was intended to exclude small vessels fishing inshore, and there was a further exemption for vessels whose voyages were of less than a week in duration, whose crew details were entered on a different, less detailed form. Crew lists were to be made out every six months, and if men left or joined whilst the list was in force the form was amended accordingly. Such was the theory, but in some places, principally the ports from which smacks fleeted, a separate list was made out for each voyage.

The front or first page of the basic crew list form sets out the particulars of the vessel (name, official number, registry port, tonnage and later the means of propulsion), the name and address of the skipper and managing owner and as far as possible the nature of the intended voyage, which normally means only that the method of fishing being conducted is entered, although some also say approximately where they intended to fish. Inside, a table gives the details of every member of the crew: name, rank, age, birthplace, name of previous ship and time and place of signing on and off, and reason for leaving. In cases where men remained with the vessel,

G. R. & R. O. OF S. & S.
RECEIVED
12 NOV 1913

[*Executed in sixteen pages.*]

S. 9.
(42 Men.)

PARTICULARS OF FISHING BOAT AND EMPLOYMENT.

ISSUED BY
THE BOARD OF TRADE,
In pursuance of
57 & 58 Vict. c. 60.

Name of Fishing Boat and Port of Registry.		Official Number.	Port—Letters and No.
S.S. Select Yarmo		139999	YH 544

Commencement of Agreement.		Tonnage.		Horse-power.
Date.	Place.	Gross.	Register.	
29 APR 1913	Gt Yarmouth	73·88	38·09	70 130

* If a Steam Ship, S.S. should be placed before the name.

RUNNING AGREEMENT,
ACCOUNT OF VOYAGES AND CREW
AND
OFFICIAL LOG BOOK
OF A
Fishing Boat of 25 Tons Tonnage or upwards
TOGETHER WITH

FORMS OF RECORD AND REPORT OF EVERY CASE OF DEATH, INJURY, ILL-TREATMENT, OR PUNISHMENT; AND OF EVERY CASUALTY TO THE FISHING BOAT OR TO ANY BOAT BELONGING TO HER.

NOTICE.—It is not necessary that Seamen engaged or discharged under this Agreement should attend before the Superintendent of a Mercantile Marine Office; but every Seaman has a right to appeal to the Superintendent if he has any dispute with the Skipper or Owner as to his wages, or his share in the profits of the voyage or a fishing catch, or any deductions therefrom, or concerning his engagement, service or discharge, or respecting the provisions. A Skipper may appeal in like manner in case of a dispute with the Owner.

On whatever date the Agreement is made it expires on the next following 30th day of June or 31st day of December, as the case may be. If, however, the Fishing Boat is absent from the United Kingdom on the 30th day of June or 31st day of December, then this Agreement remains in force until the first arrival of the Fishing Boat at her final port of destination in the United Kingdom after such date, or the discharge of cargo consequent on such arrival.

This Agreement is to be delivered up to the Superintendent of a Mercantile Marine Office on the 30th June or 31st December, as the case may be; or if the crew are at sea and serving under it on those dates, then it must be delivered to the Superintendent within 48 hours after it has been terminated by the discharge of and settlement with the crew; the Superintendent will thereupon issue the Certificate of Deposit (C.C.).

TO BE FILLED IN BY THE SUPERINTENDENT.			
Termination of Agreement.		Received at	11 NOV 1913
Date.	Place.	on the____ day of_____ 19	
30/8/13	Gt Yarmouth	by_____ Superintendent.	

V 21. Wt. 13542/87. (88). 5,000. 7/12.—McC. & Co. Ltd.—

this last is usually marked 'continues'. Apprentices were recorded separately on a space on the front of the form, with only their name and rank given.

Crew lists should give full details of how each man was to be paid. This is complicated since different systems existed, but the way in which pay was calculated should be specified on the form. In particular, if a vessel's net profits were totalled up and then divided into shares, the total number of shares should be given. For example, Humber smacks' earnings were usually divided into eight. The mate and skipper took two and a half between them, one and three eighths and one and one eighth respectively, and the owner took the rest and paid the junior crew members. All such detail should be explained on the form, although occasionally it is not. A column is given for the weekly wage: if this is blank, the man was paid only by share of the profits. The next column gives the extent of any shares, which is variously rendered as a number of

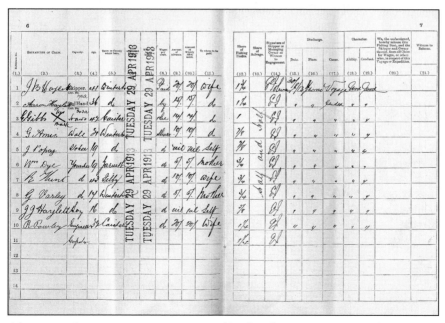

Above and opposite page: *a crew list for the Great Yarmouth steam drifter* Select, 1913. (*The National Archives, BT144/200*)

shares (if the system outlined above was used) or as a sum to be paid per pound earned by the vessel. The next column gives the amount of money, if any, advanced to the man before the voyage, which would later be deducted from his pay. Men were also entitled to make an 'allotment' of pay for their families or dependents whilst they were at sea: this is given in two columns, for the amount to be paid weekly and to whom it was to be paid, typically entered as 'wife', 'mother', 'landlady', or a named individual. Occasionally, an address is given as well.

The final two columns, after details of discharge, are for notes on the man's conduct and ability. This is usually entered simply as 'VG' (Very Good), 'G' (Good) or 'D' for 'Decline to comment', which was a polite way of suggesting that a man was incompetent or ill-behaved. This was a formality and often little attention was paid to it. On many lists the ability and conduct columns are either not completed at all or simply marked 'G' or 'VG' for the entire crew, although deserters were usually marked with a 'D' for conduct. On occasion, however, some thought evidently did go into the descriptions. In 1885, one man was dismissed from the Lowestoft smack *Caroline* for incompetence: his conduct is marked 'G,' but his ability as 'none'.

Part of the thinking behind the introduction of crew lists was that they would better protect apprentices and others against abuse, and allow for better investigation of accidents. Accordingly, all accidents, punishments and instances of misconduct or insubordination aboard the smack had to be logged in a space provided. A crew list for the Yarmouth smack *Pet* records how, 'Thursday January 14th 1886 the wind north by east laying north west by north with the sail on port side when the smack *Bonny Boys* came across our stern and luffed to leeward of us and came alongside of our lee bow and broke our bowsprit.' If men died aboard, the circumstances should be explained, and sometimes a list of the man's effects is given. This method of keeping crew lists altered only slightly during the first half of the twentieth century, and even forms from the late twentieth century are in much the same format. Numerous amendments were made, but the substance of the agreement was unchanged.

Crew lists, then, are a superb resource for researching fishing and fishermen and they contain a wealth of detail. However, not all of them survive, and those that do are distributed across a variety of repositories. Many dating from before 1913 are held in local archives in or near former fishing ports. The National Archives have produced a short guide to crew lists, including a list of local archives holding them, which can be downloaded from the website.

National institutions are the only repositories of post-1913 crew lists for both fishing craft and merchant ships. The National Maritime Museum retains approximately a 10 per cent sample of crew lists from 1861 to 1938 and from 1951 to 1976. In addition, they also have a 90 per cent sample for every year ending in 5, with the exception of 1945. These are held at an outstation, and two weeks' notice is required before consulting them. A research guide to these is available on their website. The National Archives, meanwhile, holds a 10 per cent sample of crew lists from 1861 to 1938 and from 1950 to 1994, and all surviving crew lists from 1939 to 1950. Fishing vessel crew lists are catalogued separately until 1929 in Class BT 144, in which they are sorted by ship's official number. From 1930 they are in with the main run of crew lists in BT 99, also sorted by official number. Crew lists from 1939 to 1950 are held in classes BT 380, and some may have been catalogued into BT 381. Some for 1939 to 1942 are also to be found in BT 99/7758–7815. Crew lists postdating 1990 are held at the Registry of Shipping and Seamen, and copies can only be obtained by writing to them.

All of these repositories account for about 30 per cent of surviving crew lists. The remainder for 1863–1938 and 1951–1976 were taken by the Maritime History Archive in Canada (www.mun.ca/mha). There is an online database for those dating from before 1938, searchable by vessel's official number. This will tell you if and what material the archive holds on the vessel, and you can then order copies at $2.50 per page. Some databases containing individuals' names are starting to go online. A project at the Hull and Grimsby archives has led to the names of vessels, owners and some crew members from those ports being entered into a database, which can be accessed via their online catalogues.

Finding the right list in archives can be time-consuming. In most places they are sorted by either ship's name or official number, so you really need to have this information to hand before you start searching, and be aware that men changed ships frequently. Once you gain access to the archives, you may well find that crew lists are held in boxes containing an unsorted series – for example, all of those from one year or for a run of official numbers, or both, so looking through them can be time-consuming. Many lists are in quite poor condition, and as rule nineteenth-century fishermen did not write a neat copperplate hand, so they can sometimes be difficult to decipher. Crew lists, therefore, are not without their difficulties for the researcher, but they hold more detailed information on individuals than virtually any other source and the student of fishing and fishermen is likely to have to use them at some point.

4.2 Records of apprentices

If you think an ancestor may have been apprenticed as a fishermen, or for that matter in any other maritime trade, you are in luck. There are more comprehensive records of apprentices than any other sector of the workforce, and they are easy to access and use.

The apprenticeship system in general is well covered. There is a detailed report on apprentices at Grimsby, made by an inspector from the Local Government Board, dating from 1872. A handwritten draft is in the National Archives, in class MH 32/99. There is another report, also on Grimsby, dating from 1894. This is in the parliamentary papers for that year, but a better option is the copy in the National Archives, class MAF 12/15, which comes in a box with a large file of letters, newspaper cuttings and other material relating to it. Both of these reports comment mainly on Grimsby, where the apprenticeship system was most heavily used (and abused), but most of their comments apply to other places as well. Neither of them name individuals, except that both include a list of Grimsby apprentices imprisoned in the previous year, with details of the offence and sentence.

To trace an individual, the first port of call is the National Archives. Class IR 17 contains registers of the duties payable on apprenticeship indentures between 1710 and 1811. They contain details of the master's name, address and business, together with the name and indenture date of the apprentice. Parish apprentices are not included in these, meaning that parish records, held in local record offices, need to be consulted. For more recent apprentices,

NAME AND DESCRIPTION.	DATE OF ENTRY.	1875		1876		1877		18		18		REMARKS.
		Out.	Home.	Out.	Home.	Out.	Home.	Out.	Home.	Out.	Home.	

Petrie, John
Born at *Dundee* Aged *16* Bound *12.3.75*
Registered *12.3.75* at *South Shields* Term *3* Years
To whom Bound *Laurence Smith, Newcastle.*
(Master Mariner)
Date of Entry: 1878

Procter, Frederick Turton
Born at *Nottingham* Aged *16½* Bound *13.3.75*
Registered *13.3.75* at *Hull* Term *4* Years
To whom Bound *John Gilliatt, Hull.*
(Smack Owner)
Date of Entry: 1879
Remarks: Fishing / Deserted 6.1878

Pinner, Charles
Born at *London* Aged *16* Bound *13.3.75*
Registered *13.3.75* at *North Shields* Term *4* Years
To whom Bound *John Eskdale, North Shields*
Date of Entry: 1879
Remarks: Deserted 6.1878

Phillips, Nicholas George
Born at *London* Aged *16* Bound *11.3.75*
Registered *11.3.75* at *Lowestoft* Term *4* Years
To whom Bound *Robert Stone Pinney, Southwick*
(Fisherman) (Sussex)
Date of Entry: 1879

Peacham, Joseph
Born at *Hull* Aged *17½* Bound *11.3.75*
Registered *11.3.75* at *Hull* Bound *3½* Years
To whom Bound *James Haine, Hull.*
(Smackowner)
Date of Entry: 1878
Remarks: Fishing

Pogson, Sam
Born at *Holmfirth* Aged *19* Bound *11.3.75*
Registered *11.3.75* at *Hull* Term *4* Years
To whom Bound *John George, Hull.*
Date of Entry: 1879
Remarks: Fishing / Still employed 6.1878

Page, George Charles
Born at *Lewes* Aged *17* Bound *15.3.75*
Registered *19.3.75* at *Grimsby* Term *4* Years
To whom Bound *George Jeffs Jr., Grimsby.*
(Smackowner)
Date of Entry: 1879
Remarks: Drowned at Sea 20.9.78 / Fishing

Pearce, Charles Henry
Born at *Bournemouth* Aged *15* Bound *15.3.75*
Registered *22.3.75* at *Sunderland* Term *4* Years
To whom Bound *George Watson, Sunderland*
Date of Entry: 1879
Remarks: Injured at Sunderland 30.5.77

Parratt, Thomas
Born at *Aberdeen* Aged *14* Bound *22.3.75*
Registered *24.3.75* at *North Shields* Term *4* Years
To whom Bound *John Mackenzie, Blyth*
Remarks: Cancelled (77) at N. Shields 7.4.76 Ind. rec. with V.Y. 8.6.76

Peero, Henry Walter
Born at *London* Aged *14* Bound *23.3.75*
Registered *25.3.75* at *Grimsby* Term *7* Years
To whom Bound *Thomas Ready, Grimsby.*
(Smackowner)
Date of Entry: 1882
Remarks: Fishing

Board of Trade Register of Apprentices, 1875. Fishing apprentices are usually marked in the right-hand column. Several are noted as having deserted by 1878. (The National Archives, ADMISO/45)

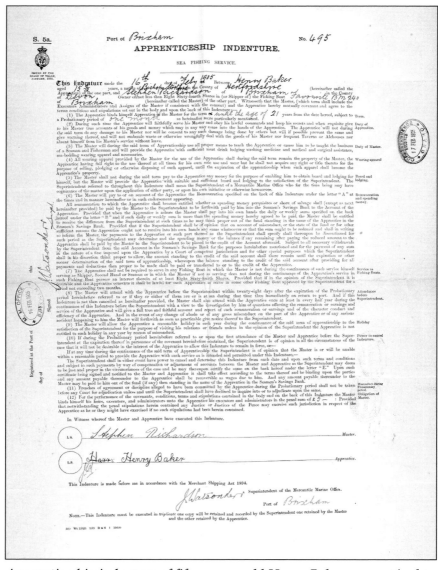

Apprenticeship indenture of fifteen-year-old Henry Baker, apprenticed to Stephen Richardson of Brixham until his twenty-first birthday. The front of the indenture sets out the conditions; on the back Baker's pay is explained. (The National Archives, BT152/3)

MERCHANT SHIPPING ACT, 1894.

ENDORSEMENTS referred to in the BODY of this INDENTURE and in the ACT.

A.

Particulars of Remuneration, viz.:

1. Spending money or allowance in the nature of wages per week during the continuance of the Indenture.

Here insert full particulars of the amounts to be from time to time paid by the Master on account of the apprentice during the term of the apprenticeship under the different heads.

The proceeds of all she crabs, oysters, and squids taken by the Boat every week to an amount not exceeding 2/6 in any one week until employed as 3ʳᵈ Hand; and when employed as 3ʳᵈ Hand, one-fourth of the proceeds of all Rays taken by the Boat and brought to market and sold, to an amount not exceeding 5/- in any one week.

2. Shares of salvage or salvage services.

A due proportion of all Salvage earned by the Boat.

3. Perquisites and other emoluments if any.

B.

Daily or Weekly sums to be paid by the Master into the hands of the Apprentice subject to the provisions of Clause 6.

C.

I hereby certify, pursuant to Section 395 of the Merchant Shipping Act, 1894, that
  (a) this Indenture complies with all the requirements of Part IV. of the Merchant ship Act, 1894.
  (b) the Master with whom the Indenture is made is a fit person for the purpose.
  (c) the Apprentice is not under the age of thirteen years and is of sufficient health and strength.
      the nearest relations of the Apprentice or his guardians assent to this apprenticeship and to the stipulations in the Indenture of Apprenticeship.
*(d) ~~no nearest relations or guardians of the Apprentice~~ {~~can readily be found~~ ~~are known~~} ~~and in their absence~~
      ~~I have acted as guardian for the occasion~~

* Strike out the words which do not apply.

Dated this 16ᵗʰ day of *Feby* 18 *1905.*

J. *Watsonder*

Superintendent.

D.

The Apprentice having this day been brought before me I hereby certify that upon full inquiry I see no sufficient grounds for interfering with this Indenture.

Dated this   .   day of   18   .

Certificate to be signed by Superintendent if Indenture not cancelled at expiration of probationary period.

Superintendent.

E.

I certify that in my opinion in all the circumstances of the case it will not be desirable in the interests of the Apprentice to allow the within written Indenture to remain in force, and I hereby cancel and determine the same accordingly from the   day of   18   (upon the terms and conditions and subject to the payments following, viz.:—

Dated this   day of   18   .

Certificate to be signed if Indenture cancelled during probationary period or upon first attendance before Superintendent.
) *Strike out the words in brackets if not wanted.*

Superintendent.

I certify that in my opinion the Master is or will be unable within a reasonable period to provide the Apprentice with such service as is intended and permitted under the within written Indenture. And I hereby cancel and determine the same accordingly from the   day of   18   (upon the terms and conditions and subject to the payments following, viz.:—

Dated this   day of   18

Certificate to be signed if Indenture cancelled on account of inability of Master to provide service.
) *Strike out words in brackets if not wanted.*

Superintendent.

the position is rather better. The Board of Trade's Registers of Apprentices, held in the National Archives, contain the basic details of every apprentice to a maritime trade between 1824 and 1953. These are in class BT 150, available on microfilm. The format varies a little, but all of the registers give the apprentice's name, dates of birth and indenture, duration of the term to be served and name and residence of master, and sometimes his occupation as well. From 1875 to 1879 the apprentice's birthplace is given, and after 1880 details of his death or the cancellation of the indenture are given, which they sometimes were before. Some of the registers provide space for voyages to be filled in, which is not always done and which usually only shows a six-monthly pattern taken from crew lists, but which may at least give you the name and number of the vessels he sailed on.

The details given in these books were transcribed from the copy of the indenture which was sent to the Board of Trade when it was signed (the local Custom House and master each retained another copy). These give a little more detail on the terms of the indenture, such as how the apprentice was to be paid and sometimes where he was to live. The National Archives holds a 10 per cent sample of apprentices' indentures for each fifth year between 1845 and 1950 in class BT 151, and a separate series for the specific Sea Fishing Indenture introduced in 1884 in class BT 152. The National Maritime Museum also holds some, as do other archives and museums, although there are often very few and they are not always in order.

Another provision of the 1883 Act was that the Board of Trade Superintendents had to keep a register of all fishing apprentices in their port. These survive for Grimsby between 1879, when a local registration scheme was set up, and 1936, in North-East Lincolnshire Record Office (class 208/1/1–11) and for Brixham between 1892 and 1912, in Devon Record Office (3287S add/6). Detail is rather sparse in many entries in the Brixham register, but the Grimsby books are a mine of information and personal detail. As well as the basic information on the apprentice they include details of where he had come from, the names of nearest living relatives and the date and reason for cancellation of the indenture, if appropriate. Meetings between apprentice and superintendent are noted, as are details of the vessels the apprentice worked on,

Entry for Robert Davies in the Register of Apprentices for Grimsby. Davies absconded in July 1886, only four months after he was apprenticed. (North-East Lincolnshire Record Office) updates on his progress and his behaviour, notes on any incidents and attempts to desert and sometimes comments or newspaper cuttings on court cases he was involved in. These registers complement the registers of apprentices kept at Custom Houses, mentioned in Chapter 2.

Records also exist of many institutions from which apprentices, and indeed other fishermen, were recruited. Parish records, held in local archives, are useful in tracing pauper apprentices. Sometimes these will include a register of workhouse inmates apprenticed in each year. Failing this, workhouse minute books and ledgers, as well as the minutes of Poor Law Guardians' meetings, will often give brief details of boys' apprenticeships. Orphanages and children's homes were a prime source of recruits, and records for many of these survive. Hull City Archives, for instance, holds the records of the Hull Mariners' Church Orphan Society, and also the Fishermen's Bethel admission registers and baptism returns, whilst North-East Lincolnshire Archives hold those for the St Anthony's Orphanage and a couple of other children's homes in the town. Access to some of these records, mainly those less than a century old, is restricted by data protection laws.

Another fertile recruiting ground was disciplinary institutions, principally reformatories and training ships. Again, the records of these will be found in local archives. To give one example, Devon Record Office holds numerous records from Whipton Reformatory, which supplied apprentices to Brixham. These include a discharge book, in which contact with former inmates was recorded. This allows you to trace the early years of an individual's career. William Smith, for instance, was discharged in June 1905, and correspondence with him is noted until November 1908, by which time he was regarded as 'a good boy', despite having served one term in prison for refusing duty. The records of several training ships also survive. Those for TS *Formidable* are in Bristol Record Office, and for *Mount Edgecumbe* in Plymouth and West Devon Record Office. Typically, these records will include lists of inmates, discharge books and disciplinary records, among other things. Again, data protection restrictions may apply to more recent records.

One final source that can be of use in tracing apprentices and sometimes other fishermen and seamen is local court records. Minor offences such as desertion or insubordination were dealt with at magistrates' courts or at the petty sessions and notes of such cases appear in the court minute books, usually held in local archives. Where desertion was very high among apprentices, cases came before court almost on a daily basis. These records are not always very complete or easy to read and often are not indexed, but they do contain a fair number of individuals' names. Seamen who fell foul of the law appear on more records than those who did not, and this is especially true of fishing apprentices, teenagers thrown into a hard occupation under a binding contract that allowed them few ways to leave without breaking the law.

Further Reading

David Boswell, *Sea Fishing Apprentices of Grimsby* (Grimsby Public Libraries and Museum, 1974)

David Butcher, *The Trawlermen* (Tops'l Books, 1980)

Edgar March, *Sailing Trawlers: The Story of Deep-Sea Fishing with Long-line and Trawl* (David and Charles, 1970)

Robb Robinson, *A History of the Yorkshire Coast Fishing Industry, 1780–1919* (University of Hull, 1987)

———, *Trawling: The Rise and Fall of the British Trawl Fishery* (Exeter University Press, 1996)

Jeremy Tunstall, *The Fishermen* (McGibbon & Kee Ltd, 1962)

Martin Wilcox, 'Opportunity or Exploitation? Apprenticeship in the British Trawl Fisheries, 1850–1936', in *Genealogists' Magazine*, vol. 28, no. 4 (December 2004)

Chapter Five

THE HERRING FISHERY AND
INSHORE FISHERIES, 1815–1950

The British herring fishery emerged in a strong position from the Napoleonic Wars, and then experienced a period of steady growth for nearly a century, rising rapidly to a peak just before the First World War, which tipped it into a slump from which it never fully recovered. The main centres of the herring fishery in the early nineteenth century were still East Anglia and Scotland, and these remained the most important areas throughout the century, although increasing amounts of herring were caught in western waters, in the Irish Sea and off the south-west of England.

The herring fishery of the east coast of Scotland began to expand early in the century, with larger boats being used, more men becoming involved, new ports such as Peterhead establishing themselves and rising amounts of cured fish being exported. This owed much to the crown brand, which guaranteed a quality cure and therefore encouraged exports, thereby stimulating the fishery even after the bounties offered for branded barrels were withdrawn in 1830. From the 1830s, prices began to rise as well, giving a further boost to the growing industry, and from here the herring industry all over Scotland expanded steadily for the next few decades. Its prosperity was based mainly on exports, in the early part of the century to Ireland and the West Indies, but with an expanding market in Europe, which by the end of the century took most of the herring exported from Scotland. By 1881, according to the Fishery

Board's annual report, the herring fishery employed 14,809 boats manned by 48,121 men, who supplied a curing industry employing another 48,752 – and in that year nearly 750,000 barrels of herring were exported.

The boom ground to a halt in the 1880s. Up to this point, crews had made agreements with curers, who took their catches at a price agreed before the season began. The advantage of this system was that it gave fishermen reasonably predictable returns for their effort, but the disadvantage was inevitably that if the price of cured fish fell during the season the curers, many of whom borrowed heavily from banks to finance the season's curing, risked financial ruin. Until the 1880s high prices and a ready export market averted a crisis, but in 1884 prices fell sharply. The fishing effort slowed down, and many curers went bust. From 1887 the system of engagements fell out of use in favour of curers buying the fish at a daily auction. The industry remained somewhat depressed for a decade or so after this crash, but when the boom resumed in the 1890s it took the fishery to an unprecedented size.

South of the border, growth was more measured. The buss fishery and curing at sea were abandoned in the early nineteenth century, and with it the system of fixed engagements with curers fell out of use in favour of auctions, three decades earlier than in Scotland. The crown brand did not apply in England and curing standards were more variable, but even so, the total amount of herring exported from the British Isles rose from around 320,000 barrels in 1853 to 660,000 in 1871, with English exports accounting for a proportion of the increase. In 1881, Lowestoft's 467 fishing vessels of all types employed around 2,600 men and Great Yarmouth's 610 boats 2,500. Another 1,700 men worked seasonally, mainly agricultural labourers who signed on for the autumn herring fishing season.

Three main developments in the fishing underpinned growth. The first was rising levels of mobility. Herring fishing had usually been seasonal, and fishermen had pursued other species in the off-season or laid up their boats, but increasingly boats and crews moved around the coast to take advantage of peak seasons in different places. By the end of the nineteenth century, some East Anglian boats were working off Scotland in the spring and working their way down the coast until the 'home season' in the autumn,

A group of onlookers watch a fleet of luggers put to sea from Newquay in the late nineteenth century. (Basil Greenhill Collection)

after which some even went on to the south-west for a winter fishery. By 1882, many Lowestoft drifters were idle for only the first six weeks of the year. It was mainly the owner-skippers and small owners who pursued these fisheries. They were risky ventures, but offered the possibility of substantial reward at a time when boats would otherwise have been laid up and not earning anything.

The migration of fishing boats was accompanied by those who gutted and packed the catch, the famous 'herring lassies'. The majority were young women from the Scottish fishing ports and, employed by the curers, they moved around the coast with the fishing fleets. Each autumn they arrived en masse in East Anglia, and usually lodged with local fishermen and others involved in the industry. No fewer than 5,000 came to Lowestoft and Great Yarmouth for the 1914 season. Few local women were employed in this part of the industry, although the herring fishery did generate a considerable amount of employment in making and maintaining nets, and in some of the smokehouses.

The herring lassies worked in the open air in teams of three, two gutting the herrings with a deft flick of the knife and then passing them to a third who packed them into barrels and sprinkled them with salt. Each team could handle up to 20,000 herrings a day. It was a tiring job, working in the open air for long hours in all weathers, but many of those who did it remember it with affection. 'It was such fun,' one lady commented, and many people remarked on the herring lassies' high spirits and habit of breaking into song, often a hymn, whilst working.

The second development was the lengthening of the fishing season. The customary 'herring season' represented the time when the best, fattest fish were caught, but 'spent' fish could be had at other times of the year. During the nineteenth century, a summer herring fishery opened up off East Anglia. The fish caught were thin and not of great quality, but they could be sold profitably for farmers' manure. Much the same happened elsewhere.

Thirdly, herring began to be caught further offshore. Until then most herrings had been taken within ten or twenty miles of the coast, but by the end of the nineteenth century vessels were fishing up to fifty miles out. Larger and more seaworthy boats were necessary for this, and various types were developed. Until the 1850s, all Scottish herring vessels were open boats, but decked vessels came into use from the middle of that decade. Famously, the 'scaffie' and 'fifie' were developed in Scotland, both of them lug-rigged craft but with different hull forms, the scaffie having a shorter keel and raked stem and stern. In the late 1870s, the 'Zulu', named after the Zulu War then being fought, was created, combining the best features of both types. This was the classic Scottish herring drifter, and hundreds were in service by the turn of the century. Decked boats were already in use south of the border, but they became larger over time, and from the 1870s the lug rig was replaced in some areas with ketch rig, or 'dandy', as it was known, which was not as powerful as lug rig, but broke the sail plan down into smaller units which were easier to handle.

From the 1860s, too, machine-made cotton nets came into use. These were lighter and stronger than the old hemp nets, and so larger 'fleets' of nets, up to two miles long, could be used, and steam capstans were introduced to speed up the handling of them. As aboard trawlers, steam capstans were not always popular with crews because 5 per cent of vessels' earnings were allocated for their maintenance. Resistance to steam capstans even went as far as rioting on occasion, but the efficiency gain they promised was too big to ignore, and eventually they became standard equipment. Thanks to increasing numbers of larger boats using longer and lighter nets, the catching power of the British herring fleet expanded fourfold between the 1850s and the 1880s.

The next great innovation was steam power, which came to drifting later than to the white fisheries. The first steam drifter was named *Consolation*, reputedly because of the full sailing rig it carried in addition to its engines. It entered service at Lowestoft in 1897, and was an immediate success. By 1913 there were about 1,800 at work. Sailing drifters hung on at the smaller ports, but the major ports of East Anglia and Scotland replaced their fleets of luggers with steam drifters. In contrast to the trawl fishery, however, this did not trigger any great move towards company ownership of boats. Drifters were smaller and simpler than trawlers, and although a steam drifter was a lot more expensive then a lugger it was not beyond the means of a successful individual, and most drifters continued to be owned by

A steam drifter enters Great Yarmouth, circa 1900.

their skippers. Steam drifters could, of course, reach the fishing grounds in weather too calm for sailing vessels and catch far more fish, so rising costs were offset by greater profits.

Larger boats needed better harbour accommodation, which in many areas was a serious problem. Many Scottish fishing stations had harbours far too small to accommodate all of their boats, or very difficult to get into when the weather was bad. Disasters were inevitable. On 19 August 1848, a violent storm hit northern Scotland and, although the fleets ran for shelter, many could not enter safe harbours. More than 100 men died that night. Afterwards, efforts were made to improve harbour accommodation, although it always struggled to keep pace with the growing numbers of boats to be housed. Many harbours were very congested, especially during the herring season. Even so, improved harbour accommodation was central to the growth of the British fishing industry as a whole in the nineteenth century.

Herring fishing, for the crews, was very hard work. There was no place aboard a drifter for someone who would not – literally – pull their weight. 'Chuck 'em out. Sack 'em … I believe that every time a man ain't no use, don't carry him,' one former East Anglian drifterman said, summarizing the general attitude amongst crews. Drifting was intensely competitive, as each boat sought to make the largest catches possible and be first back to secure the best prices at auction. Sometimes, drifters were driven harder than was safe. As much sail as could be carried was crowded on, and several steam drifters were lost when engineers, many of whom had had no formal training and learned their craft on agricultural traction engines, tied down safety valves to increase power, sometimes resulting in a boiler explosion. But the attraction of drifting was the money. A farmhand who signed on to an East Anglian drifter for the autumn season could double his annual farming wage in a few months, and the skilled full-time workers in the crew, who took a larger share of the profits, earned more still.

Boats went out in the evening, arriving on the fishing grounds as darkness fell and the shoals rose closer to the surface. The nets were 'shot' immediately and then the crew had chance for a meal and some rest. Accommodation aboard drifters was not exactly generous – one small cabin for the crew, no sanitary facilities and only basic food – but voyages were short so this mattered little. Every so often, the net was brought in a little and, once the skipper judged that there was enough fish in it, the hard work of hauling in up to a mile of nets began, taking each net off the head rope as it came aboard and 'scudding' the fish out of it. As soon as the nets were in, the drifter made for port as fast as she possibly could, with men on deck still separating fish from nets, repairing any damage and setting the gear up for the next night's fishing.

The British herring fishery peaked in 1913. In that year, British drifters caught just less than 600,000 tons of herring worth nearly 4.5 million pounds. During the autumn season, 1776 drifters, 614 local and the rest mainly Scottish visitors worked from Great Yarmouth and Lowestoft alone. At that time, there were more than 8,000 full-time fishermen at the two ports, and around 1,300 seasonal workers.

There were no plans to use drifters for naval service when the First World War broke out. It was expected that trawlers, which were built for towing and therefore ideal minesweepers, would be sufficient. However, it soon became apparent that there was a need for small patrol vessels, a role for which drifters were suitable, and many were thereafter requisitioned. Those that remained fishing were severely restricted in their activities on the east coast, and activity switched to the south and west. Many driftermen went into the naval reserve.

After the disruption and losses of the war, the trade expected a return to normality, but this was never to happen. There was a brief recovery, but then the fishery slumped as political upheavals in Russia and central Europe closed off the biggest export markets, and prices for British herring plummeted. There was a short recovery in the 1920s, and then a second and worse slump that lasted for much of the 1930s. Throughout the interwar period the herring fishery had too many vessels chasing too small a market, making a loss but owned by men unwilling to sell them because they were now worth less than the mortgages taken out to buy them. Men stuck with fishing, too, because often there were few other jobs available. Landings fell on average by 12 per cent annually during the 1930s, and by 1938 they had dropped to 330,000 tons; not much over half the level of 1913.

There were a few encouraging developments. Drifters powered by internal combustion engines, which were cheaper to buy and to run than steam engines, started to be built. The Danish seine net was introduced as well, which allowed some drifters to fish for other species in the off-season for herring. This was not enough to halt the decline, though, and in 1935 the Herring Industry Board was set up to reorganize the industry. It offered loans for replacing old and inefficient boats, sought out new markets and encouraged development of new methods of preserving and marketing the product. None of this had time to bear much fruit before war broke out again in 1939, and again fishing in the North Sea and many other areas all but ceased. So the immediate priority once wartime price controls were removed, vessels readied for work and men released from military service, was to continue the reforms that had begun in the 1930s. As it happened, they were to be overtaken by events beyond the control of the Herring Industry Board or anyone else.

Historically, most fisheries have been conducted inshore, in the sense of being close to the coast, and it is really only in this period that people began to distinguish them from the great offshore sea fisheries, albeit with some difficulty. A report from 1914 defined an inshore fisherman as follows:

> He as a rule goes out either for a day or a night's fishing; he usually fishes from his own boat, which is of limited dimensions and without steam power, fishing within sight of land, although not necessarily of home; and he also carries on all those fisheries which do not in all cases require the use of a boat, such as fishing with stake nets and the gathering of shellfish by hand.

This is a fair summary and, as it suggests, the term inshore fishing covers a wide range of activities. From beaches all around the coast of Britain, small boats of various sorts caught a variety of species, often rotating their activities with the seasons. From Thorpeness, Norfolk, in the late nineteenth century men fished for crabs and lobsters in the spring, used small trawls for plaice and soles or shrimps in early summer, and then drift nets for herring in the autumn before laying their boats up for the winter.

Oyster dredging aboard the Mayflower *in the early 1950s.*
(Basil Greenhill Collection)

As the comment above suggests, there were also many fisheries that did not involve going to sea at all. Shellfish continued to be gathered in many places, perhaps most notably Morecombe Bay, and cockles and oysters from the Thames and along the south coast. There were also fisheries involving weirs and traps of various kinds, such as the 'brat-nets' set up in estuaries for turbot, or the 'stake-nets' used on beaches in the north-west. There were even a few who used explosives to kill fish in inland pools, which could then be gathered by hand, until this practice was banned in 1877.

There were also several important fisheries in estuaries. One notable example is the 'stow-boat' fishery for sprats pursued in Essex, especially at Leigh and Southend. Stow-nets were stocking-shaped much like trawls, except that they were worked from smacks anchored in the path of a moving shoal. The smacks were small, fast cutters, also used for oyster-dredging in the off-season. In the late nineteenth century, some were also hired out as carriers for the North Sea fleets. Many of their crews made a second income

A party of day trippers are about to put to sea in a coble at Filey, on the Yorkshire coast, in 1892. (Basil Greenhill Collection)

in the summer season out of crewing aboard yachts, where their seamanship, honed by years of negotiating tricky waters in all weathers, was much in demand.

Much of what has been said of inshore fisheries before continued to apply well into the twentieth century. Many inshore fishing stations were small and isolated towns and villages and produced only a small amount of fish for market, which was usually sold locally. Fishing was often combined with other activities such as farming or, in the south and east, smuggling. The communities centred on fishing were generally tight-knit and self-reliant, with fishing families marrying amongst themselves and sons following fathers to sea. Boats were owned by working fishermen, and those who worked them were paid a share of the catch.

Stephen Reynolds described life in the small Devon port of Sidmouth at the turn of the twentieth century, where he spent much time living with the Woolley family (for whom he used the pseudonym Widger) in the small cottage in which they lived, amid a warren of ancient streets populated mainly by families connected in one way or another with fishing. He wrote thus of the fishing one autumn:

> There has been no fishing. Either the sea has been too rough to ride to a slingstone [a heavy stone used instead of an anchor] for blinn and conger, or else too calm, so that the mackerel hookers could not sail out and therefore no fresh bait was to be had. It is quite useless to fish for conger with stale bait. Tony tells me that I ought to be here in a month's time, when he will have fewer pleasure parties to attend to, and will go out for mackerel, rowing if he cannot sail. He says there will have to be a good September hooking season, because, though the summer has been fair, the fisherfolk have not succeeded in putting by enough money to last out the winter, should the herrings fail to come into the bay, as they have failed the last few years.

As this passage suggests, the fishing itself was heavily seasonal, with a winter herring season complementing summer fishing with lines ('hooking') and nets for mackerel and other species. It was at times a precarious existence, especially when the herring shoals failed to appear, and inshore fishermen of Sidmouth and elsewhere supplemented their income from fishing by taking parties of tourists on pleasure trips, sometimes combined with a little sport fishing.

Isolation was a feature of inshore fishing ports, but the coming of the railways did link some of them into the national market for fish and allow them to benefit from the generally rising incomes and levels of prosperity of Victorian Britain. Even a small station like Hornsea, in East Yorkshire, where a few cobles worked from the beach, catching crabs, herring and cod depending on the season, could send upwards of fifty tons of fish a year inland by rail by the 1880s. Thanks to easier and cheaper transport, many inshore stations began to send most of their fish to market. This gave rise to occasional complaints about rising prices locally, and it often spelled an end to ways of selling the catch that had stood for centuries. The 'jowders' or 'jowsters' of Cornwall, who hawked fish around inland towns on foot, largely disappeared after the railway bridge over the Tamar was completed in 1859, allowing fish to be sent profitably to much larger markets further afield.

Although this was not always a benefit to the rural poor near the fishing ports, it did mean that fishermen could earn more money, and indeed the nineteenth century was a prosperous time for most of the British fishing industry. It was not without its problems, though, and some of these were to grow more and more serious as time went on. Pollution was one such issue. The pollution of the Thames, so bad that the smell famously caused Parliament to close in the summer of 1858, had already killed off the live cod trade in London, and it also affected the oyster beds further downriver. Many became polluted with sewage or industrial waste, and around the turn of the twentieth century there were several typhoid outbreaks caused by contaminated shellfish from several sources. The most notorious was in 1902, when the Dean of Westminster died after a banquet in Winchester. Typhoid was said to be the cause, probably contracted by eating contaminated oysters from Emsworth in Hampshire. The Emsworth fishery never recovered.

As the fishing industry grew, so did conflicts between different users of the fishing grounds, especially those close inshore. Trawlers cut through the nets of drifters and swept away long lines, which men of small means could ill afford to lose. Nor did they have much of a way to recover their losses. They could take legal action, but this was expensive and inconvenient and often not worth the effort. The problem worsened for inshore men on the east coast when converted paddle-steamers began to be used in the late 1870s for trawling close inshore. Various rules were introduced to keep trawlers and other vessel separate, but none of them was completely

A visiting Flemish fisherman, photographed at Brixham between the wars. (Basil Greenhill Collection)

successful, even when District Sea Fisheries Committees were set up to regulate fishing in coastal waters.

Some fisheries failed from natural causes. For reasons that have never been fully explained, the pilchard shoals around the south-west coast moved further offshore in the late nineteenth century, and from the 1870s the ancient seine fishery slipped into decline. At St Ives, the biggest seining centre, the number of registered seines fell from 286 in 1869 to only thirty or so by the early 1900s. Pilchards were still caught, but the picturesque seines died out in favour of small wooden drifters, or 'drivers' as they were known locally.

Many of these were motor-powered, and this was the main innovation in inshore fishing in the first half of the twentieth century. Internal combustion engines had the same advantages to inshore men as others, and although some were reluctant to adopt them – such as those Stephen Reynolds knew at Sidmouth – between the wars motorization took off, and made fishing boats both more efficient and safer. Powered gear, such as equipment for hauling in long-lines, also increased efficiency. Often, traditional boats could be adapted to take engines and many were so modernized. Indeed, motorized versions of some very old fishing boat types still exist today.

5.1 Ship registers

Tracing the registry of a fishing vessel is useful to the family historian for two reasons. First, details of the ship he worked aboard can give you a much clearer picture of what your ancestor's working life involved. Secondly, knowing the registration details of a ship makes it much easier to find certain other records, such as crew lists. Fishing vessels were usually registered and recorded with merchant ships, but separate records also exist and can be a very valuable source for tracing individual vessels, especially those that for one reason or another – mainly through being very small – escaped recording in the main series of documents.

By the Act for the Increase and Encouragement of Shipping and Navigation of 1786, all British ships of more than fifteen tons' burthen with a deck (in other words, not open boats) had to be registered with Customs officers in their home port. Many particulars about the ship had to be recorded, but most importantly:

- Port registry number
- Name of ship
- Home port of ship
- Date and place of registration
- Owners' names, addresses and occupations
- Date and place of building (or capture, if it were a prize of war)
- Key dimensions – length, breadth, depth and tonnage
- Number of decks and masts
- Name of master

These details were entered into a register at the Custom House, and a copy known as a transcript was sent to the Custom House in

Form No. 9.

CERTIFICATE OF BRITISH REGISTRY.

PARTICULARS OF SHIP.

Official Number of Ship.	Name of Ship.	No., Date, and Port of Registry.	No., Date, and Port of previous Registry (if any).
76913	Cricket	Peel	Nil

Whether British or Foreign Built.	Whether a Sailing or Steam Ship, and if a Steam Ship, how propelled.	Where Built.	When Built.	Name and Address of Builders.
British	Sailing	Peel Isle of Man	1867	Henry Graves, Peel Isle of Man

		FEET	TENTHS
No. of Decks	One		
No. of Masts	Two		
Rigged	Dandy		
Stern	Elliptic		
Build	Carvel		
Galleries	None		
Head	None		
Framework	Wood		

	FEET	TENTHS
Length from fore part of Stem under the Bowsprit to the Aft side of the Head of the Stern Post	48	5
Main breadth to outside of plank	13	6
Depth in hold from Tonnage Deck to Ceiling at Midships		
Depth in hold from Upper Deck to Ceiling at Midships in the case of Ships of three decks and upwards		
Length of Engine Room (if any)		

PARTICULARS OF ENGINES (if any).

No. of Engines.	Description.	Whether British or Foreign made.	When made.	Name and address of Makers.	Diameter of Cylinders.	Length of Stroke.	No. of Horses power (nominal)

PARTICULARS OF TONNAGE.

	In Register Tons	In Cubic Metres		No. of Tons.
GROSS TONNAGE			DEDUCTIONS ALLOWED.	
Under Tonnage Deck			On account of Space required for propelling power	
Closed in Spaces above the Tonnage Deck			On account of Spaces occupied by Seamen or Apprentices, and appropriated to their use, and kept free from Goods or Stores of every kind, not being the personal property of the crew.	
Space or Spaces between Decks				
Poop				
Forecastle			These Spaces are the following, viz. :—	
Round House				
Other Closed in Spaces, if any, as follows				
GROSS TONNAGE		85.52		
DEDUCTIONS, as per Contra		Nil		
REGISTER TONNAGE		85.52	TOTAL DEDUCTIONS	

I, the undersigned Registrar of Shipping at the Port of _Peel_ hereby certify that the Ship, the Description of which is prefixed to this my Certificate, has been duly surveyed, and that the above Description is true; that _James McCarthy_ whose Certificate of Competency or Service is No. _Nil_ is the Master of the said Ship; and that the Name, Residence, and Description of the Owner and Number of Sixty-fourth Shares held by _him_ are as follows:

Name, Residence, and Occupation of the Owner.	Number of Sixty-fourth Shares.
James McCarthy of Sherkin Island in the County of Cork Thomas McCarthy of Sherkin Island in the County of Cork Seamen and Fishermen Joint Owners	Sixty fourth 64 ths

Dated at _Peel_ the _23rd_ Day of _June_ One thousand eight hundred and _eighty one_

George Wood Registrar of Shipping.

London, via Edinburgh in the case of Scottish ships. Since this only applied to larger, decked vessels, many fishing boats were excluded. Virtually all inshore craft and many of the offshore herring fleet, certainly, were too small or undecked. On the Yorkshire coast, for instance, cobles were not registered whereas 'five-man boats' were. No separate provision was made for registering fishing boats, so those that were registered were recorded with the main run of merchant ships.

All the Transcripts at Custom House in London were destroyed in a fire there in 1814, so the National Archives holds no ship registers for ports other than London from before this date. Many do survive for other ports, however, and can be found at the relevant local record offices. From 1814 onwards, the registers at the National Archives can be found in class BT 107. This class is arranged by region and indexed in class BT 111, which contains two series, one sorted by ship's name and the other by official number, and is available on microfiche.

Under the Merchant Shipping Act of 1854, which consolidated and tidied up various existing laws, responsibility for administering shipping was transferred to the Board of Trade, and the system of maintaining registers was changed, starting from 1855. Transcripts and Transactions, the records of vessel ownership, were separated. Transcripts can now be found in BT 108 and Transactions in BT 109, again both indexed in BT 111. The information contained is much the same as before, although more detail was included on ships' propulsion, because of the increasing number of steamships coming into use.

From 1890, the system changed again and reverted to keeping all papers together. These can be found in class BT 110, sorted by the date the ship's registry was closed. Therefore, to find details of a ship in this class you need to know the date it was lost, sold abroad or broken up. It is important to be aware of the fact that some registries were reopened, say if a ship was sold abroad and then bought back, and in these cases the papers will be entered according

Opposite page: *Certificate of registry for the* Cricket, *built at Peel on the Isle of Man, and registered at Skibbereen, County Cork, in 1881. (The National Archives, BT100/20)*

to the date of the final closure. This system ran until 1994 when the registry system was computerized. A series of registries still open at this date, arranged by ship's name, is in BT 340.

Such was the system for merchant vessels and larger fishing boats. However, a more detailed registration system including much smaller fishing craft was introduced under the Sea Fisheries Act of 1868, with the intention of giving a more detailed picture of the national fishing fleet. Under this act, all fishing vessels of any size required registration with the local Custom House and were assigned a port registration mark which they were required to display clearly at all times. From here come the distinctive combinations of letters and numbers carried by British-registered fishing vessels down to the present day. A list of port markings can be found in Appendix 2.

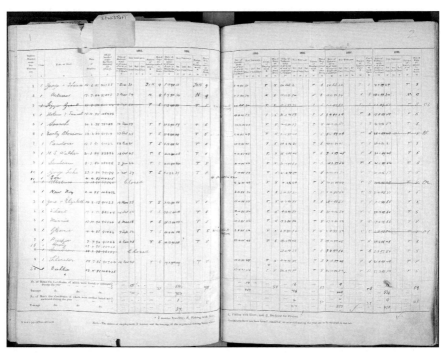

Page of the Register of Fishing Vessels for the port of Lowestoft, 1893–8. (The National Archives, BT145/2)

Also under the 1868 Act, fishing boats were divided into three classes. First-class boats were those over fifteen tons, second class those smaller but powered by means other than oars, and third-class boats were powered by oars only. Those second and third class boats whose tonnage was unknown were classed by the length of their keels. First-class boats and some second-class were large enough to fall under the Merchant Shipping Acts, and transcripts of their registries were sent on to London and can be found in the records described above as well as in local Custom House registers; most second and all third class boats are in Custom House registers only. The system was modified slightly in 1877 to exclude from registry altogether open boats working within three miles of the coast, so very small boats disappear from the registers thereafter for everywhere except Ireland, where the exemption did not apply; Scotland's exemption was cancelled in 1880. Abstracts of numbers of boats in each class at each port can be found in the Annual Statements of Navigation from 1871 onwards.

The Merchant Shipping Act of 1894 established a national system for registering fishing vessels, based on annual returns sent in by each Custom House.

The registers thus generated are in class BT 145 at the National Archives. They are sorted by port, with vessels listed in order of their port number. The entry for each fishing boat contains:

- Port number
- Class
- Name
- Date of registration
- Official number
- Tonnage
- Date and reason for closure of registry

From 1934, each ship's net tonnage, the number of men needed to work it and a very brief abbreviation of the nature of its employment are also given. The importance of BT 145 is that it links together a ship's port number and its official number, which makes it easier to locate records sorted by official number in archive catalogues. The national registers of fishing craft cease in 1938, after which the researcher is again dependent on locally held records for all except larger fishing boats. Several archives, however, hold port registers of fishing vessels up to the late 1980s. Some port records, too, go back before 1868, meaning that, although it was not a legal requirement to keep such information, some very small fishing vessels may be traceable.

Apart from official records, fishing vessels appear in a few other places. Publications such as *Olsen's Fisherman's Almanac* sometimes give lists of boats, as occasionally do books and pamphlets covering local maritime industries. Fishing vessels registered under the Merchant Shipping Acts appear on *Lloyd's List*, the list of British ships published by Lloyd's of London. A complete set of these is available in the Caird Library at the National Maritime Museum, the Guildhall Library in London, and other specialist libraries also hold sets. Some ports published annuals, mainly as a means of advertising but also to serve as directories, which again sometimes include vessel lists. These will normally be found in local studies libraries. For the port of Brixham, Mike Miller has transcripted the registers of fishing and other vessels at the port from 1784 to the present day. Copies are available at Brixham Heritage Museum.

5.2 Certificates of Competency and Service

In addition to the introduction of crew lists and regulations relating to apprentices, another provision of the Merchant Shipping (Fishing Boats) Act of 1883 was that skippers of fishing vessels larger than twenty-five tons had to hold an official Certificate of Competency. Before this, in fact, trawler skippers had frequently been certified by port insurance clubs, but these were administered by smack-owners and it was strongly felt that this system lent itself too well to abuse. Consequently, the 1883 Act placed the power of granting certificates in the hands of the Board of Trade.

Certificates of Competency were granted on the basis of an examination, which was made more difficult and more theoretical over time as the average level of education among applicants rose and as vessels became larger and more complex. Those who could prove

REMARKS.	NAME.	AUTHORITY No.	AUTHORITY Grade.	Where born.	Year.
Cert. Cat. on Thain'og. 13. 1st Cefy 26.7.16	Cowie George	1571	SK 17.9.10 Buckie.	Buckie	1869
En 3 nb/19 Cerhy lost overboard 21/2/19 in the Dardanelles. New granted 16/4/9	Thompson James	2	SK 9.6.10 Yarmouth	Catfield Norfolk	1882
29/10/19 Fined £1 and costs for unlawfully serving as Skipper of the "Ocean Dawn" without being duly certificated M 10871/19.	Green George William	3	SK 2.6.10 Yarmouth	Caister Norfolk	1893
Has Skprs 9c 13566	Ritchie Alexander King	4	SK 11.6.10 Aberdeen	Collieston Aberdeen	1870
Authority lost 30/9/11 New authority 3639 sent to Yarmouth 6.10.1911	Barnard Henry Barney	5	SK 24.5.10 Yarmouth	Caister Norfolk	1844
	Thain Alexander	6	SK 13.6.10 Wick.	Ackergill Caithness	1861
	Bush James	7	SK 28.5.10 Yarmouth	Pakefield Suffolk	1867
En 23 31/1/18 Cerhy lost through enemy action. New Certy issued 26.1.19	Brown Edward	8	SK 3.6.10 Yarmouth	California Norfolk	1868
	Cowie James	9	SK 7.3.11 Buckie	Buckie	1865
	Bosworth Frederick	1580	SK 29.6.10 Yarmouth	Gorleston Suffolk	1873

Register of Certificates of Service for skippers and mates of fishing vessels, 1914–9. (The National Archives, BT130/5) prior service as a skipper did not have to take an examination, but were granted a Certificate of Service instead. From 1886, the system was extended to second hands (mates) as well. In both cases, the certificate could be suspended for incompetence or misconduct, which debarred the holder from serving in his previous capacity.

The indexes of these certificates are held in the National Archives in class BT 138: there are three of them only, for names beginning A–F, F–O and O'H–Z. The index will give you the number of the individual certificate, which then allows you to go to the Registers. These are BT 129 (Certificates 1–15,509) and BT 130 (01–07884). They are kept on microfilm only, although the National Maritime Museum holds some of the originals, including some very early ones from Grimsby, where the scheme was piloted in 1880. They are sorted by certificate number.

Each certificate contains the individual's name, place and year of birth and place and date at which the certificate was awarded. In addition, some detail is given of each certificate holder's voyages, although this is patchy and not always reliable. Details of the individual's death are sometimes given, especially if he died at sea, and if the certificate was suspended for any reason or the holder convicted of an offence this is noted as well. Yarmouth skipper John Edmonds was convicted in November 1889 of failing to exhibit the compulsory navigation lights at night and fined £2, whilst three years later he was 'severely censured and reprimanded' for being absent from his vessel at sea for a whole night. If you are trying to trace someone who served, or may have served, as mate or skipper of a fishing vessel, the Registers of Certificates of Competency are very easy to use and potentially very valuable.

5.3 Scottish fisheries records

Fisheries have been, and are, more important to the economy of Scotland than the rest of the British Isles; and Scotland has retained separate, or at least semi-separate, political, administrative and legal systems. As a result, for large parts of its history the Scottish fishing industry has generated a separate body of records. Most of these can be found at the National Archives of Scotland.

As mentioned above, there were various attempts to encourage the herring fisheries in the eighteenth century, mainly by means of bounties on fish caught. The earliest surviving records generated by these are in the Customs records of the Exchequer. They are vouchers for payments of bounties to herring fishing vessels between 1752 and 1796, arranged by port and vessel name. They are very useful because, as well as describing the boat and outlining what she caught and where, they give names, birthplaces and descriptions of the crew. For those interested in that industry, whalers are also included. The vouchers can be found in class E 508, and they correspond to entries in the Cash Accounts in class E 502.

Another attempt to stimulate activity came from the British Fisheries Society, a joint-stock company mainly composed of landlords and merchants, which sought to develop the western Highlands by creating or expanding fishing stations. The records of the Society from 1773 to 1877 are in class GD 9, including the central administrative papers and letters, and records for Tobermory, Lochbay, Pulteneytown and the only notably successful settlement, Ullapool.

The solution for the Scottish herring fishery finally came when the Fishery Board was established in 1809, again paying bounties to herring boats and also establishing the Crown Brand. The Board remained in existence, although reorganized, until 1939, when its responsibilities were transferred to the Secretary of State for Scotland and remained there until 1991 when it passed to the Scottish Office as the Scottish Fisheries Protection Agency. Following devolution, responsibility for fisheries passed to the Scottish Environment and Rural Affairs Department. Records relating to fisheries from the late eighteenth century (there is some material predating the Board) to 1999 are in series AF at the National Archives of Scotland.

Classes AF 1–5 contain central administrative records including minutes and out-letters, the corresponding in-letters for which are in AF 37–8. AF 14–36 contain detailed reports of fishing in the districts administered by the Board, weekly and in some cases daily, giving quantities of fish landed at each station, numbers of boats working and miscellaneous observations by the district officers on the weather, market prices and other matters affecting the fishing. Annual reports on the fishing from 1809 to 1980 are in AF 82.

Unfortunately, few boats or individuals are named in these reports, although many contain other sundry material which may be of interest. Other useful material can be found in AF 56 and AF 64, which contain details of illegal fishing and offences against fisheries laws between 1882 and 1960, and AF 62, which includes papers on a variety of topics including unemployment amongst fishermen and emigration dating from between 1816 and 1986. As will be obvious from this brief survey, this is a very large archive indeed containing a wide variety of material covering a long period of time. Parts of it still await detailed research, and more valuable sources may well come to light.

In addition to the Fishery Board records in series AF, there are also some papers relating to fishing in class NG 1, the records of the Board of Manufactures, which was responsible for fishing before 1809 and retained some responsibilities after then. NG 1/65 has miscellaneous papers relating to fishing dating from between 1765 and 1851, which mainly seem to relate to exports and to the cod and ling fisheries. Some of this material is very detailed, such as reports by masters of long-line vessels from 1819 to 1820 (NG 1/65/3), which include names of masters and some others as well as details on where and how they fished and what was caught. NG 1/6 contains letter books relating to fishing from 1848 to 1868. The National Archives of Scotland also holds records from the Sea Fish Industry Authority and White Fish Authority from the second half of the last century, but access to these is restricted. Some of this material will probably be duplicated at the National Archives.

Various other repositories hold collections of records that relate to fishing. The National Library of Scotland holds papers from Richardson and Company, who were involved in salmon fishing, mainly as buyers, in the late eighteenth century. The documents relate mainly to fishing around the Tay. The Shetland Archives have the records of curers Thomas Adie and Sons, including fishing agreements, dating from 1888 to 1902 and some other miscellaneous records. Finally, the archives of many port towns and counties containing fishing stations – in Scotland and elsewhere – hold the records of port authorities, which may possibly include material on fishing vessels. However, enquiries to local record offices would be needed to confirm this.

5.4 English fisheries records

There was no equivalent of the Fisheries Board south of the border. However, there are some records of regional fisheries administrations in England, as well as some interesting material in the archives of the Board of Trade.

The Fisheries Department of the Board of Trade was set up in 1886 to monitor the industry and to administer some of the regulations introduced under the Fishing Boats Act of 1883. It took over some powers previously held by the Home Office. It had only a small staff, and its existence was short, for in 1903 it was absorbed into the Board of Agriculture and Fisheries, a predecessor of the Ministry of Agriculture and Fisheries.

The records of the Fisheries Department are held at the National Archives, in class MAF 12. The most significant individual item is the report on the apprenticeship system from 1894 (MAF 12/15), discussed in Chapter 4, but there is much more. While the items do not appear to have been sorted into boxes by subject, so papers relating to particular matters can be found in several different ones, the online catalogue gives a useful summary of the contents of each. Most material relates to offshore trawl and drift-net fisheries, although there is correspondence on matters such as lights and harbour accommodation that is germane to all parts of the industry.

In the first instance, there are numerous papers relating to administrative matters. For example, in MAF 12/10 and 16 there are reports and regulations pertaining to fishing in the territorial waters of other nations, for which several vessels were arrested. There are also a couple of reports. MAF 12/12 contains a brief report on the apprenticeship system at the ports of Great Yarmouth and Lowestoft, whilst MAF 12/2 includes two short reports regarding the fishermen's reaction to the 1886 Fishing Boats Act, which was not well received in several ports, as well as the extent to which the rules applied to different classes of fishing boat.

There is also a considerable amount of correspondence with local Board of Trade officers who had requested clarification on particular rules. For instance, in MAF 12/14 there is correspondence dating from 1894 with the superintendents at various ports regarding apprentices, including summaries of the differing methods by which they were paid and general remarks on the effectiveness of the rules introduced during the previous decade. As another example, MAF 12/20 contains correspondence with Hewett & Co at Great Yarmouth, regarding the employment of non-apprenticed boys under the age of 16.

Most interesting, however, are several records of prosecutions of fishermen, apprentices and fishing vessel owners under the Fishing Boats Acts, and it is here you will find the greatest number of named individuals. To give two examples, a bundle of papers in MAF 12/2 relates how Grimsby smack-owner John Gidley was prosecuted and fined after he twice refused to attend the Board of Trade office regarding a dispute over wages with a crewman named George Peters, and then 'appeared at the office in a most abusive manner, cursed and swore, and said he positively refused for the Board of Trade, or anyone else, to attend at the office.' At the other end of the scale, there is a file of newspaper cuttings and responses from Board of Trade officials in MAF 12/1 relating to the prosecution of Hull apprentice Henry Dalton in 1887 for refusing to put to sea, which was of interest to the Fisheries Department because of a dispute over whether under the Fishing Boats Acts the stipendiary magistrate had the power to cancel indentures of apprenticeship. The Fisheries Department archive, then, is quite miscellaneous in its contents, but it is small and well catalogued, and certainly worth investigation. Records generated after 1903 are discussed in section 6.1.

A possible source of information on English inshore fishing is the records of Sea Fisheries Committees. These were established under the Sea Fisheries Act of 1888, which established the framework in which committees could be formed to regulate fishing in their area. Over the next decade, several such committees were formed and by the early twentieth century most of the coast of England and Wales was under their jurisdiction. Operating under the control of the Board of Trade, they had wide-ranging powers to restrict or ban any method of fishing within their area, make rules on the size of nets and their meshes, constitute oyster beds and prohibit the discharge of harmful substances. They could impose fines for breach of these rules. District Sea Fisheries Committees still operate, although their powers have been modified by successive Acts of Parliament. Most maintain websites, which give a general introduction to their work.

Many Sea Fisheries Committee records are not available for research and many records less than thirty years old remain closed, but some of the earlier records have been transferred to local archives. They are rather variable in content, but most extant archives contain committee minutes, and some also include correspondence. Periodically, some Sea Fisheries Committees conducted surveys and censuses of fishing activity in their area, which can sometimes be found, and some of their records will include notes on offences against local by-laws. Sea Fisheries Committees produced annual reports. Some can be found with other papers in local archives, and some are in MAF 209 at the National Archives.

Further Reading

David Butcher, *The Driftermen* (Tops'l Books, 1979)

Peter Frank, *Yorkshire Fisherfolk* (Phillimore & Co Ltd, 2002)

Malcolm Gray, *The Fishing Industries of Scotland 1790–1914: A Study in Regional Adaptation* (Oxford University Press, 1978)

Trevor Lummis, *Occupation and Society: The East Anglian Fishermen 1880–1914* (Cambridge University Press, 1985)

Edgar March, *Sailing Drifters: The Story of the Herring Luggers of England, Scotland and the Isle of Man* (Percival Marshall & Co, 1952)

Cyril Noall, *Cornish Seines and Seiners* (D. Bradford Barton, 1972)

Stephen Reynolds, *A Poor Man's House* (John Lane, 1908)

Paul Thompson, Tony Wailey and Trevor Lummis, *Living the Fishing* (Cambridge University Press, 1983)

Chapter Six

THE BRITISH FISHERIES SINCE THE 1950s

Since the 1950s, there have been fundamental and far-reaching changes in the fishing industry. In most respects it has developed and become more efficient, in some it has become a victim of its own success and in others it has been influenced, sometimes damaged, by factors beyond its control. Fishermen now pursue species that were previously left alone, on grounds not formerly fished, using very sophisticated technology to hunt down fish that are becoming increasingly scarce and operating in an industry and a market determined by complex and sometimes ineffective legislation.

There is no escaping the fact that as a whole the fishing industry has declined in the last half-century, especially in the 1970s and 1980s. In 1967, there were 23,782 full- and part-time fishermen in the United Kingdom; by 1997 this had dropped to 18,604 and by 2006, the last year for which figures are available at the time of writing, to 12,934. Figures for the total number of fishing boats are hard to ascertain because of changes in how vessels are defined, and small boats sometimes escape counting altogether, but the number of vessels over forty feet in length fell from 2,131 in 1967 to 1,594 in 1997. In 2006 there were reckoned to be 6,372 fishing vessels of all types in Britain, down from 8,073 in 1996. Total fish landings fell from over a million tons per annum in the 1950s to 614,000 in 2006.

Fishermen work to supply a market. Demand for fish and its by-products from consumers, as well as how the market is organised to supply them, have both changed a great deal in the last fifty years. The old methods of curing pelagic fish are gone, the distribution

The harbour at Girvan, Ayrshire, in the late nineteenth century. It is crowded with herring luggers, most of the smaller, open type then being replaced with larger, decked boats. (Basil Greenhill Collection)

system for fresh fish that grew up in the nineteenth century has broken down and the famous fish trains from the big ports have been replaced by refrigerated lorries. By 1997, we were eating half as much fresh fish as thirty years previously, and twice as much processed fish. Rather than coming from the port, to one or two wholesale markets and then onto a fishmonger's counter, much of the fish we consume now is brought by large processing firms, sometimes employing boats on contract to fish for them exclusively, and then sold on through a few giant supermarket chains. The old trade in fresh fish still exists, but the traditional fishmonger and even the fish and chip shop are threatened species. Despite this, consumption of fish in Britain has been rising since the 1970s. Fish is seen as a low-fat alternative to meat, and as it has become more fashionable so species not previously eaten in Britain have begun to be caught or imported by air freight. The fish trade, like most others, is now a global business.

The technology of fishing has advanced at a startling rate over the last half-century. Until only a few decades ago, fishing vessels were mainly navigated in very traditional ways, with compass and chart, and finding fish depended entirely on the skill of the skipper and his knowledge of the fishing grounds. Electronics have revolutionized this part of the industry, with Global Positioning Systems (GPS) allowing much more precise navigation, and ever more sophisticated equipment being devised to locate fish. Engines have also become much more powerful, and the introduction of powered blocks has allowed much larger nets to be handled. The cotton nets which supplanted handmade hemp nets in the nineteenth century have themselves been replaced by those made of artificial fibres, which are stronger, lighter and require less maintenance. Fishing methods have changed too. To take the example of trawling, standard trawls are still very much in use, but new forms have been introduced, such as pair-trawling and beam-trawling, using outrigger booms aboard the trawler to hold the mouth of the net open. Some beam trawlers operate two trawls, one on each side.

Little of this was apparent in the early 1950s. The fishing industry was much as it had been in the 1930s, although smaller in scale. The distant-water fishery, in particular, was starting to look old-fashioned despite the large new motor trawlers coming into use. Part of the problem, in fact, was that these were updated version of pre-war designs rather than the new form of factory stern-trawlers that were being developed, especially in the Eastern Bloc states, where massive investment was being directed into the fisheries.

There had been some experiments with factory vessels in Britain before the war, when Hellyer's of Hull and Bennett's of Grimsby fitted out three former refrigerated meat transport vessels to catch and freeze halibut off the coast of Greenland. The experiment was a partial success, but it was not followed up. Christian Salvesen & Co of Leith, already world leaders in factory whaling ships, experimented with stern trawling in the late 1940s and placed an order for the first British stern trawler, *Fairtry*, which entered service in 1954. *Fairtry* was far larger than existing trawlers and carried a crew of eighty, four times that of a contemporary side trawler, in much more comfortable accommodation. Working conditions were also safer and less arduous, since a stern trawler did not have to turn broadside-on to the weather to haul the trawl, and the gutting and sorting of the catch could be carried on in a sheltered space, rather than on the open deck. She was capable of freezing thirty tons of fish daily and carrying 600 tons of frozen fillets.

Impressive though *Fairtry* and two similar vessels which entered service with Salvesen's a few years later were, they were not without teething problems and they were very expensive to build and operate. As a result, during the 1950s most British trawler owners persisted with traditional side trawlers, which in addition to the dangers of hauling the net in over the side were also constrained by the lack of equipment for freezing fish at sea, which limited them to trips of around three weeks' duration, fishing the established grounds off Iceland, Norway and the Soviet Union.

Access to some of these waters was beginning to be disputed. The

Exactly the same location as the previous picture, photographed in 1987. The sails are gone but, as the two boats in the foreground suggest, wooden hulls along traditional lines were built until after the Second World War. (Basil Greenhill Collection)

Icelandic government was concerned that overfishing would damage the cod stocks upon which its economy depended, and in 1958 it extended Iceland's territorial waters from four to twelve miles, sparking off the first of what became known as the Cod Wars. Icelandic gunboats tried to arrest British trawlers fishing within the twelve-mile limit, whilst their skippers attempted to outmanoeuvre the gunboats and get back to the protection of British naval vessels. Occasionally shots were fired, and several trawlers were rammed by gunboats, and vice versa. The dispute ended in a settlement in Iceland's favour after two months, but flared up again in 1972 when the Icelandic limit was extended to fifty miles. This time the dispute was more bitter and dragged on for a year, with British trawlers managing limited fishing under protection of frigates, before a temporary agreement was reached. When this expired three years later, the Icelandic government extended the limit again to 200 miles. The British government refused to recognize this, and in November 1975 the Third Cod War broke out. This lasted until the following June, when the British government agreed to withdraw trawlers from Icelandic waters altogether. Cold War politics played a major part in the incident, with the base at Keflavik, south-west Iceland, crucial to NATO's presence in the northern seas. British withdrawal was partly occasioned by a threat to close the base.

The end of the Third Cod War was also the end for much of the British distant-water fishing industry, and the fish docks at some of the principal ports fell silent. As the biggest distant-water port, Hull was hardest hit and today has only a handful of trawlers. Other ports such as Grimsby had retained near- and middle-water vessels, but they too suffered badly. Thousands of men were thrown out of work and, since they were technically casual labourers, until the late 1990s they received no compensation at all. Britain still has a small fleet of factory trawlers, working in some of the deepest seas in the world to supply the international market.

With the distant-water fishery in decline, the British fishing effort switched back to home waters. Here, it has to contend with the twin problems of severe overfishing, and political strategies to control it. Overfishing is not a new problem. As we have seen, even by the late 1870s the North Sea was showing signs of overfishing, when it was worked only by small sailing vessels with, by modern standards,

Mending nets is one job that still has to be done by hand, as the crew of the Banff-registered Prowess *demonstrate, at Ullapool in 1997. (Basil Greenhill Collection)*

tiny trawls. In 1998, the preserved Lowestoft smack *Excelsior* was fitted with a replica of the type of beam trawl used in the late nineteenth century and did some experimental fishing in the North Sea. She caught nothing, in a striking if not very scientific display of how much more serious the situation has become.

Since the war, not only demersal fish stocks have become depleted. The long-established method of fishing for herring with drift nets came to an end during the 1950s and was replaced with much more efficient mid-water trawling and seine netting. Catches increased, peaking in the late 1960s, and then began to decline as the stock became more and more depleted until it collapsed in 1977 and the fishery had to close altogether. The stock has recovered since and the fishery reopened cautiously in 1981, but overfishing of herring remains a problem to this day.

To manage the developing overfishing problem and to resolve disputes between European countries over rights of access to fishing grounds, the European Community established the Common Fisheries Policy (CFP) in 1971, and Britain became subject to this when she joined in two years later. From 1974, a system of Total Allowable Catches (TACs) was used to limit the amount of fish that could be taken from different areas of European waters. This is still in force today, albeit with many modifications over the last thirty years. The proportion of the TAC for each species that each country and fishing vessel can take is determined by a system of licences to fish, along with which comes a quota that can be taken. As fish stocks have become more depleted, so quotas have been reduced and schemes set up to encourage the scrapping of vessels, and to help fishermen switch to different species or to leave the industry altogether. There are also regulations on types of gear that can be used and the size of nets' meshes.

Many commentators regard the Common Fisheries Policy as a failure. Although the British fishing fleet, along with that of most other European nations, has shrunk in size, most of the vessels that have been scrapped are older and less efficient, although some fishermen have exploited loopholes in the regulations to fit out older boats with the latest catching technology. Either way, the catching power of the fleet has not diminished, and as a result over-fishing has become steadily worse. It does not help the situation that, under the CFP's rules, fish caught over and above a boat's quota cannot be landed, leading to the ridiculous situation of good catches having to be thrown back, or landed illegally. This too is a persistent and serious problem: in the early 2000s, it was calculated that perhaps half of all cod landed in Britain was over-quota and therefore illegal, or 'black' fish. Different management regimes in use elsewhere in the world have mechanisms to accommodate the fact that fishermen do not always catch what they intend to and therefore sometimes catch beyond their quotas. The CFP, however, is said to have too many players, and too many people involved with a vested interest in maintaining the status quo, and therefore is difficult to reform effectively. Moreover, no politician wants to be seen to sign the death warrant for large parts of the fishing industry by enforcing the drastic cuts in quotas that fisheries scientists argue are necessary. As fisheries economist David Whitmarsh comments, there is little sign that the CFP has delivered the 'prosperous, stable and sustainable' fishing industry that it promised. As fish stocks in home waters have become depleted, so more and more fish is imported to make up the shortfall. If you buy cod from the local fish and chip shop today, it is quite likely to have been flown in from Iceland.

Despite stock depletion and political difficulties, home waters still supply a good proportion of Britain's fish. The North Sea is still an important source, and fishing activity off the west coast has also increased. In particular, the West Country ports of Plymouth, Brixham and Newlyn are now among the largest fishing ports in the country, where trawlers pursuing cod in the eastern Atlantic are based. In Scotland, Peterhead and Fraserburgh are the largest ports, the base for many vessels working in the North Sea. Recently, several Scottish fishermen have switched to catching langoustines, for which prices are high. The North Sea is also an important area for catching crabs, lobsters and other shellfish, the largest amount being landed at Bridlington, on the Yorkshire coast.

Much of the British fishing fleet is still owned by small firms or by owner-skippers and crewed largely by young local men, prepared to work very hard in return for more money than they can make in the jobs available to them ashore. In some areas, especially in the south-west and Scotland, there are relatively few opportunities locally beyond fishing or seasonal work in the tourist trade. Small wonder many decide to go into fishing, although many also drop out in the early stages, finding the work too hard and the time away from home too long. More recently, an increasing proportion of crews in some ports have been made up of immigrants, often of east European origin, which has not always been popular with locals. Many skippers have taken out large mortgages to buy their boats and need to make a good return on their investment. The incentive to work as hard as possible, pushing vessels and crews to the margins of safety to secure a good catch is the same as ever it was. As a result, news stories about lost and missing fishing boats are still common. Nor is the danger confined to sea fisheries. The

Gathering shellfish in The Wash, circa 1900. The harvesting of shellfish by hand continues to this day.

cockle fishery in Morecambe Bay is today worked largely by immigrant labour. It hit the headlines in February 2004, when a gang Chinese cockle pickers were trapped by the rising tide and twenty-three drowned.

Britain still has an active, in some cases thriving, inshore fishing industry based at many ports around the coast, and many long-established inshore fishing grounds are still exploited. Much inshore fishing is seasonal and a part-time occupation for many fishermen, and its contribution to total fish landings in Britain is small, but it is often important to the local economy. Inshore fishing is not affected by the Common Fisheries Policy, so long as it is conducted within Britain's twelve-mile limit. However, increasing pressure on some fish populations, especially in Scotland, has led to the introduction of new regulations to conserve stocks.

Inshore fishermen are less able to shift their catching areas to follow the fish and so, as has been the case for centuries, much inshore fishing is still seasonal. Fishing from the beach still continues in many places, mainly for shellfish. On the Yorkshire coast, cobles can still be found at work, usually fishing for shellfish. Modern cobles are powered by engines rather than oars and sails, and they are hauled up the beach by rusting tractors instead of hand capstans and horses, but the basic design is still at work. In other places, traditional forms of fishing vessel have been replaced by more modern ones but doing a similar job.

Hastings remains the largest fishing centre in Britain without a harbour. The traditional sailing craft have long gone, replaced by a fleet of small motorized vessels for fishing in the English Channel, which are still launched from the beach, fishing for soles and plaice in the spring, lobsters and crabs in the summer and cod in the winter. The Hastings fleet has been praised for its sustainable fishing practices, and others comment favourably on the local Fisheries Protection Society, which allocates berths on the town's beach, runs the fish market and facilities such as net-making and supply of boxes to the boats and promotes the fishermen's interests to the local authority and to the wider public. Hastings may represent the future of British fishing; a small-scale venture catching a high-quality product in sustainably small quantities – but even here there are problems. In January 2008 the Fisheries Protection Society mounted a campaign against the latest round of cuts in the cod quota, which threaten to close the winter fishery altogether, perhaps making the difference between survival and bankruptcy for some of the boats. Here as elsewhere, conservation and the interests of the fisherman do not always coincide.

These are changing times for the British fishing industry. The decline of the 1970s to the 1990s, which swept away most of the distant water fishery and other long-established fisheries such as North Sea herring drifting, is largely over, and in some places fishermen are doing well for themselves again, albeit in smaller numbers than before. In many places around the coast, fishing is still recognizably the business that it has been for generations, from the locality of the men and the types of boats and gear used, to the species being caught and sold. These are also uncertain times, however. Overfishing and cuts in quotas are still driving many out of the industry, or forcing them to change working practices that in some cases have been established for many years. A Fisheries Research Service survey amongst Scottish fishermen in 2001 found that many were concerned about the future of the industry and their own place in it, felt that it would consist in future of fewer but more efficient vessels and were unhappy about the effect of the industry's shrinkage on the economies and communities of the towns in which they lived. The fishing industry down the centuries has changed dramatically in response to demand from consumers, cultural habit, technological developments, legislation and the ingenuity and sheer hard work of those who make their living from it. That process is far from finished yet.

6.1 The White Fish Authority and Herring Industry Board

The Herring Industry Board and the White Fish Authority were set up in response to depression in two of the most important parts of the industry, the herring fisheries in 1935 and the trawl fishery in 1950. Under the control of the Fisheries Board of the Ministry of Agriculture and Fisheries, both sought to develop their respective sectors, promoting their products and providing money for investment in more efficient boats and equipment. They were merged in 1981 into a non-departmental body, the Sea Fish Industry Authority, or Seafish (www.seafish.org).

Their papers are the National Archives, in class MAF 209. Most of the papers relate to scientific research, legal matters and investment. Numerous reports were produced on new vessels, fishing gear and methods of processing. MAF 209/72, for example, contains reports on the trials of *Fairtry* and an earlier experimental freezer trawler *Fairfree*, whilst MAF 209/153 has reports from 1949 of experimental fishing carried out by the research vessel *Ernest Holt*. Records from Fisheries Laboratories are in MAF 336, 339 and 342.

Among the White Fish Authority and Herring Industry Board papers there are numerous legal papers and sets of rules and regulations, ranging from papers dating from 1948 to 1949 on a dispute over fishing in Norwegian territorial waters in MAF 209/173–5, to new by-laws for Bridlington harbour in MAF 209/105. In terms of investment, there are papers discussing money for harbour repairs or improvements for Brixham, Scarborough, Polperro and Mevagissey, among others. MAF 209/893–5 consider loans for building or reconditioning boats. Maps and plans of estuary fisheries and harbours are in MAF 71.

MAF 209/24–9 includes papers regarding the call-up of fishermen for National Service. Finally, there are administrative records, including papers on the setting up of the White Fish Authority, appointment of members and, from 1976 to 1980, reviews of the work of both bodies. Papers from the Ministry of Agriculture, Fisheries and Food, dating from 1979 to 1985, regarding the restructuring of the industry are in MAF 452.

Both departments also published annual reports, which should be available in some local studies or academic libraries, and a few are also in archives.

6.2 Business records

'Business records' is a broad heading. It covers a variety of documents ranging from the extensive archives of large trawler firms, records of business associations and sundry other items generated by a wide range of individuals and companies involved in all aspects of the fishing industry. Most are to be found in local record offices, with some in local studies libraries and museums. A majority date from the second half of the nineteenth century and later, as business became more regulated and more reliant on the written record, but there are some fascinating survivals from earlier times. Generally speaking, company papers are not particularly helpful for tracing individual fishermen, for whom records such as crew lists are a better source of information, but they are useful for finding individuals working in the landward side of the industry, such as merchants. Many business records, searchable by trade, are enumerated on the National Register of Archives (www.nationalarchives.gov.uk/nra).

The largest company archives are those of the major trawling firms that were established in the late nineteenth century, especially in the Humber ports. The records of several such firms can be found in archives at Hull and Grimsby covering the period from the 1890s to the 1970s. Some records of owners of offshore fishing vessels other than trawlers can also be found. Suffolk Record Office, for example, has the archives of Lowestoft Steam Herring Drifters Lts, dating from 1897 to 1914, whilst archives of firms that owned herring drifters and some of the seining companies are in Cornwall Record Office. A few such records have been used to inform published company histories.

The core of these archives are usually annual accounts and directors' minute books, which deal with the day-to-day operation of the company as well as larger issues such as decisions to invest in new boats or facilities. Records of shareholders and share dealings often feature. There are also often extensive collections of letters and records of dealings with other businesses, such as fish merchants and various suppliers. The archives of many larger firms will include material relating to companies bought out by them. Records less than thirty years old are often subject to closure.

Individual fishermen appear comparatively rarely in company archives. Some collections do include settling sheets, the profit and loss account for a trip, which will name at least the skipper, and there are also some wage books, but these will mainly cover the landward staff. Company papers, then, are a particularly good source of information on people other than fishermen working for fishing firms, such as engineers and, of course, company directors.

Oyster fishing also generated some large archives dating considerably further back than most. Canterbury Cathedral Archives has a great many records of the famous Whitstable Oyster Fishing Company dating back to the early eighteenth century. The core of this archive, as with others, is the minutes and accounts. There is also a very large amount of correspondence on a wide variety of topics and, perhaps most valuable of all, records of individual oyster fishing craft, complete with names and wages paid to crews.

In many ports, numerous business associations were, and are, set up to promote the interests of groups of companies, allow them to present a united front to others and sometimes to organise services. In the many ports there were associations of fish merchants, which organised services such as the allocation of selling pitches, supply of boxes and suchlike. Since fish merchants were often one-man businesses that generated few records, these can be very useful for tracing individuals, especially since many association archives include lists of members.

On the other side of the industry, there were also federations of vessel owners, and many of these spawned mutual companies owned among their members which provided essential services. A very famous example is Cosalt, today a supplier of marine safety equipment but which began life in 1873 as the Great Grimsby Coal, Salt and Tanning Company, providing supplies of coal, salt and the material for tanning sails to Grimsby smack-owners. Some early records of this firm are in North-East Lincolnshire Archives, along with records of the Trawler Owners' Club. Other archives hold similar material.

The big collections of company and association records apply principally to the largest ports, but for many places there are a large

Lobsters being sorted into boxes, c.1955. Note the men smoking whilst working, something definitely not allowed today!
(Basil Greenhill Collection)

number of miscellaneous business records. Many of them are one-off survivals and they are by no means comprehensive, but they are a most useful resource, especially for researching inshore fishing. A large proportion of these records are financial records of one sort or another: accounts, mortgage agreements and deeds. Cornwall Record Office, for example, has account books for some of the seining companies dating back to the eighteenth century. Many more are letters, in some cases dating back to late medieval times, although most survivals date from the seventeenth century and later. Berwick upon Tweed Record Office has extensive papers of the local Salmon Fishing Company from the seventeenth to the twentieth centuries.

These miscellaneous business records, then, vary enormously in size and detail, and consequently in usefulness to the family historian. Tracing individuals in many of them is for obvious reasons rather a 'needle in a haystack' job, but if you know roughly where and when an ancestor worked and want to find out about what his working life involved and what sort of a living he made from it, these are a rich and fascinating source of information.

There are, of course, many company and business archives which have not been deposited with public archives, and remain either in private company archives or in the hands of descendants and therefore are not available for research.

Although it is not a company as such, the Royal National Mission to Deep Sea Fishermen, as it is now known, has been a constant presence in the fishing industry since the 1880s, providing spiritual and practical support to fishermen and their families. Its archives, dating back to 1886, include meeting minutes, correspondence and assorted other material. They are held at the Mission's head office in Fareham, Hampshire. Contact details can be found at www. fishermensmission.org.uk.

6.3 Newspapers and the trade press

Newspapers are the most valuable source of contemporary comment on the fishing industry, as well as a key resource for those seeking information on particular incidents. These began to be regularly and systematically published in the eighteenth century but really took off from the middle of the nineteenth, as the development of the railways and the electric telegraph made transmitting information easier, cheaper and faster. After this, a distinction quickly emerged between the national titles such as *The Times*, regional papers such as the *Western Morning News* and local and town newspapers. This distinction persists, although many of the regional titles, such as the *Eastern Morning News*, are no longer published.

The national newspapers are unlikely to be of much use to the family historian unless an ancestor was involved in a particularly major incident, and even then local coverage is often more detailed. The Bill Papper murder in 1882, for instance, provoked pages of coverage in the local press from the time the story broke, including detailed accounts of the arrests of Brand and the third hand of the smack, interviews with Papper's father and Brand's wife and verbatim accounts of the court proceedings, whereas *The Times* published only a few short reports on the trial of Brand. It is, then, to regional and local newspapers that the researcher should turn first, where you are likely to find four types of useful information.

First, there are general columns on the local fishing industry, especially where it was growing fast, or alternatively when it was in difficulties. For example, the *Grimsby Observer* published a three-part series on the growth of the fisheries in 1872, talking about the port's facilities, its fishing vessels and its fishermen. It is not completely accurate in every detail and it certainly smacks of self-promotion, but as a summary of the industry at an early state of development, it is a rare and valuable piece of work. Smaller but similar pieces were published elsewhere to mark the opening of new docks or the establishment of railway connections, and can be an interesting source of detail.

More common are records of accidents and disasters or, more positively, record catches and heroic deeds. Losses of fishing vessels usually merited an article in the local press, often naming the crew and, in the twentieth century, accompanied by photographs. More positively, the *Hull News* reported at length in December 1887 of the rescue of survivors from a sinking steamship by the Hull trawler *Lena*, and similar stories can often be found in local papers from around the country.

The local press of the nineteenth century reported court proceedings in much more detail than today. Apprentices and other men who deserted their duty or committed other misdemeanours frequently found their cases reported in the local press, as did vessel owners who went bankrupt or became involved in wage disputes with their crews. Cases of deserting apprentices, which were very common, usually merited a few lines explaining roughly what the offence was, any significant evidence given and the court's verdict and sentence. Similar information is given for other petty crimes, and major crimes or incidents such as the Great Gale of 1883 generated large numbers of column inches locally, as well as articles in the national press. Meanwhile, bankruptcy cases tend to give a potted history of the bankrupt's financial dealings, which can be very interesting.

There is also the trade press, which is often highly technical but includes more detailed commentary on the state of the industry at a given time than is available elsewhere, as well as articles on losses of vessels, notable deeds by individuals and so on. *Fishing News*, which started in 1913, is still the main title. The *Fish Trades Gazette* is also worth examination, especially for information on the landward side of the business. The same publisher produces an annual guide to the industry and directory of vessels. There is also the Mission to Deep Sea Fishermen's journal, *Toilers of the Deep*, published from 1884 to 1990 and, in Ireland, the *Irish Skipper*.

Local studies libraries invariably hold collections of newspapers, often dating back well into the nineteenth century and occasionally earlier, and those that are not held locally can be found in the British Library's Newspaper Archive at Colindale, North London. In addition, local museums sometimes hold collections. All of these are free to access, although for Colindale you will need a British Library reader's ticket. How newspapers are kept varies from place to place. Some libraries can produce the originals, which are sometimes in poor condition, but in many instances you will find they have been microfilmed to save on space and prevent deterioration.

Increasingly, old newspapers are becoming available via the Internet. Old editions of *The Times* from 1785 onwards are now online at http://archive.timesonline.co.uk/tol/archive. This is a subscription service, albeit with a free trial period, and similar services are offered by certain other newspapers. In addition, many local history websites contain transcriptions or scans of newspaper articles of local interest, although the coverage is very patchy.

The biggest problem with newspapers, though, is simply the size of the task in hand. Nineteenth-century newspapers were printed in neat columns of closely packed small type, which is not broken up with pictures in the way modern papers usually are, which slows down the search. Remember also that, even if you are searching for records of one particular incident, you may need to look through several days' editions of more than one title. Obviously, this can be a rather laborious job and you need to have a very clear idea of what you are looking for and when it happened before you approach it.

6.4 Directories

The telephone directory might not seem an obvious source for family history, but directories of various sorts are in fact very useful. Trade directories for major towns began to be published in the late seventeenth century, and from the late eighteenth century the number and coverage of directories grew rapidly as commerce expanded.

Information in early directories was collected in a variety of more or less systematic ways, but by the nineteenth century firms such as the ubiquitous Kelly's kept large amounts of information on businesses and produced updated local directories on a regular basis. The publication of trade directories peaked after 1850, remained high for the best part of a century thereafter, and then declined from the 1950s as telephone directories replaced them. Some directories were trade-specific, but many more were general local directories covering a more or less wide geographical area.

General directories usually consist of three main elements. Firstly, there is a more or less comprehensive (and reliable) directory of local services and officials and sometimes a guide to local landmarks as well; secondly a business directory arranged by trade, and thirdly a directory of private residents arranged either alphabetically by surname or by street.

Directories are most useful for tracing employers, rather than employees. Fishing vessel owners are invariably listed in the business directory for port cities, with a home or business address, but non-owners are not listed and the residential sections cover household heads only, much like modern telephone directories. Therefore, if an ancestor was a deckhand living in lodgings he is unlikely to appear in a directory, whereas a smack-owner with his own house very probably will. It is as well to check several directories if possible, since not all of them were comprehensive and you may find individuals listed in one and not another. Nevertheless, directories can be very useful for corroborating information gleaned from other sources, such as the census or crew lists.

Local studies libraries frequently hold extensive collections of directories. Increasing numbers are also being transcribed and placed on the Internet, many of them on genealogy websites. There is also a searchable database of directories for England and Wales maintained by the University of Leicester at www. historicaldirectories.org. This mainly focuses on directories from

Wooden motor vessels in the foreground of this quiet scene at Wick in 1997, with larger trawlers tied up in the background. (Basil Greenhill Collection)

the 1850s, 1890s and 1910s, although there are some others on there as well. The project that led to this valuable resource being created has now finished, and it will not expand any further. Nevertheless, it is well worth a look.

6.5 Personal papers, memoirs and contemporary commentaries

Fishermen are not noted for their introspection or for writing a great deal about their working lives, even if they can, which, since until a century or so ago most were illiterate, was not often. As a result, there are very few places from where we can get direct comment or memoirs from fishermen in even the recent past. There are exceptions, however, and the few published fishermen's diaries are well worth seeking out.

The two main ones I have used both relate to the North Sea fisheries of the late nineteenth and early twentieth centuries. Grimsby skipper Edwin Green Smith kept a diary of the voyages he made aboard several long-lining smacks between 1884 and 1888. Mostly, his diary includes technical details of how and where he fished and what was caught, expressed in his curious English. For instance, he refers to 'anlins', meaning hand-lines, and frequently complains about fish being 'all heds' when recovered, meaning that dogfish had eaten the cod once they were hooked and left only the heads. There are also a few incidents noted, such as when the mate 'pulled his thum all but of' in an accident with the winch. More detailed than Smith's log is that of John Glanville, who was a skipper with the Hull boxing fleet. It covers the period 1920 to 1925, giving details of courses, weather and catches, as well as a potted account of how much each trip made. On 3 August 1923, for example, he writes:

> Left fleet on 13th and arrived home 14th [July]. Thick fog. Made £822 and stoped (sic) home to go through [the ship's annual] survey. Ship in dock till the 25th Saturday. Expenses 256.

Both of these diaries were published by local organizations, Grimsby in the case of Smith, Hull Maritime Museum for Glanville. Both are currently out of print, but they are not difficult to find, and if an ancestor of yours worked in those fisheries, copies are worth seeking out.

There are, of course, unpublished collections of personal papers, which can usually be found in some local archives. To give two examples, the personal papers of Charles Horn, a trawler skipper at Grimsby, dating from 1902 to 1934 are in North-East Lincolnshire Archives, whilst the Brynmor Jones Library at the University of Hull holds the papers of skipper Christian Agerskow. Some collections of skippers' personal papers include settling sheets, making it possible to assess how much they earned.

More recently, the memoirs of several former fishermen have been published. Two examples are Rob Ellis's *Arctic Apprentice* (Highgate Publications, 2007), which is a pungent and sometimes hilarious depiction of its author's early years aboard Hull trawlers in the 1950s, and Paul Greenwood's *Once Aboard A Cornish Lugger* (Polperro Heritage Press, 2007), which tells of life and work on the surviving Cornish luggers in the 1960s, alternating drift-netting and long-lining as the season dictated. Increasing numbers of similar books are coming out, reflecting growing interest in the subject and in local history in general. The local history sections of libraries and bookshops are well worth a browse.

A related source of information is sound archives. Over the years, various researchers have conducted interviews with former fishermen. Essex Record Office has the tapes of interviews with several fishermen conducted in the 1970s and 1980s, North-East Lincolnshire Archives and Northumberland Archives Service possess several similar recordings, and there are numerous others in local libraries and archives. Information from interviews has been used to inform various books. In particular, many of the works of Trevor Lummis and David Butcher are heavily based on oral testimony and give transcripts of interviewees' recollections.

Contemporary observation by outsiders to the industry is also very valuable. It contains the small details that really allow the researcher to build up a detailed picture of an ancestor's working life, and sometimes home life as well. Just as importantly, it gives you some idea what outsiders thought of them and how they appeared to others. A variety of works on many different fisheries at various times have been published.

Many of the noted commentators from the seventeenth and eighteenth centuries mentioned fishing for one reason or another, such as Daniel Defoe and Tobias Gentleman. Far more comment, however, dates from the late nineteenth century and after. Ebenezer Mather founded the Mission to Deep Sea Fishermen in 1884, after seeing at first hand the conditions that North Sea smacksmen worked under. Mather, an evangelical Christian, felt it was his duty to do something to improve their lot, and worked tirelessly to publicize his cause. His book, *Nor'ard of the Dogger*, was published in 1888. As well as relating how he became involved in the fishing industry, and making many suggestions for how readers could help with his work, his account gives a great deal of sometimes stylized but interesting comment on working conditions in the North Sea Fleets.

At the other end of the industry, the work of Stephen Reynolds has already been mentioned. Reynolds, an affluent Londoner with connections to the Bloomsbury set, spent a great deal of time living with the Woolley family in Sidmouth, and his writings stand as an affectionate but honest portrait of inshore fishermen in the southwest around the turn of the century.

To this day, journalists and travel writers continue to go to sea with fishermen and record their experiences, both as television programmes and books. There have been numerous television broadcasts depicting life and labour in the fishing industry, notably the recent BBC series *Trawler*. On the Nation on Film section of the BBC website there is also an archive of film clips showing fishing during the twentieth century, including very rare clips dating from before the First World War. These can be found at http://www. bbc.co.uk/nationonfilm/topics/fishing.

In print, travel writer Redmond O'Hanlon's *Trawler* (Hamish Hamilton, 2003) vividly describes a trawling trip in the North Atlantic. *Life on the Edge: At Sea with British Fishermen* by journalist Quentin Bates (Hutton Press, 2001) describes voyages with fishermen from Whitby, Hastings, Leigh-on-Sea, Fraserburgh and Newlyn, giving an insight into the diversity that to this day is such a feature of the fishing industry, and the hard work and dedication of those who make a living from it.

Further Reading

Quentin Bates, *Life on the Edge: At Sea with British Fishermen* (Hutton Press, 2001)

Charles Clover, *The End of the Line: How Overfishing is Changing the World and What We Eat* (Ebury Press, 2004)

Appendix One

MUSEUMS AND ARCHIVES WITH COLLECTIONS RELATING TO FISHING

These are the main national repositories: for county and city archives, contact details can be found through the ARCHON directory, maintain by the National Archives, at www.nationalarchives.gov.uk/archon.

The National Archives
Ruskin Avenue, Kew, Richmond, Surrey, TW9 4DU
020 8392 5200
www.nationalarchives.gov.uk

National Archives of Scotland
HM General Register House, 2 Princes Street, Edinburgh, EH1 3YY
0131 535 1314
www.nas.gov.uk

National Archives of Ireland
Bishop Street, Dublin 8, Ireland
+353 (0)1 407 2300
www.nationalarchives.ie

British Library
96 Euston Road, London, NW1 2DB
020 7412 7676 (general enquiries)
www.bl.uk

British Newspaper Library
Colindale, London, NW9 5HE
www.bl.uk/collections/newspapers.html
(This repository is due to close during 2012, and its contents will move to the main British Library site at St Pancras)

National Library of Scotland
George IV Bridge, Edinburgh, EH1 1EW
0131 623 3700
www.nls.uk

General Register Office
Postal address: PO Box 2, Southport, PR8 2HH
Search room: as per National Archives
www.gro.gov.uk

General Register Office of Ireland
General Register Office, Government Offices, Convent Road, Roscommon
Tel: +353 (0) 90 6632900
www.groireland.ie

General Register Office (Northern Ireland)
Oxford House, Chichester Street, Belfast, BT1 4HL
028 90 252000
www.groni.gov.uk

General Register Office for Scotland
New Register House, Edinburgh, EH1 3YT
0131 334 0380
www.gro-scotland.gov.uk
www.scotlandspeople.gov.uk

Museums

Please note that this list is not exhaustive and that other local history and maritime museums hold collections relating to fishing. Preserved vessels are not listed here, although some of the museums listed have one or more historic vessels. Web links are correct at the time of writing. Many smaller museums are only open part time: you are advised to check opening hours before visiting.

Aberdeen Maritime Museum
Shiprow, Aberdeen AB11 5BY (Aberdeenshire) Scotland
01224 337700
www.aagm.co.uk

Scottish Fisheries Museum
St Ayles, Harbourhead, Anstruther, Fife KY10 3AB, Scotland
01333 310628
www.scotfishmuseum.org

North Devon Maritime Museum
Odun House, Odun Road, Appledore, Bideford, N. Devon EX39 1PT
01237 422064
www.devonmuseums.net

Arbroath Signal Tower Museum
Signal Tower, Ladyloan, Arbroath, Angus DD11 1PU, Scotland
01241 875598
www.angus.gov.uk/history/museums/signaltower/default.htm

Bridlington Harbour Heritage Museum
Harbour Road, Bridlington, East Yorkshire YO15 3AN
01262 608346

Brightlingsea Museum
1 Duke Street, Brightlingsea, Essex CO7 0EA
01206 303286
www.brightlingsea-town.co.uk/history/museum.htm

Brighton Fishing Museum
201 King's Road Arches, Brighton, East Sussex BN1 1NB
01273 723064
www.sussexmuseums.co.uk/brighton_fish.htm

Brixham Heritage Museum
The Old Police Station, Bolton Cross, Brixham, Devon TQ5 9SQ
01803 856267
www.brixhamheritage.org.uk

Buckhaven Museum
Buckhaven Library, 3 College Street, Buckhaven, Leven KY8 1LD, Scotland
01592 412860
www.fifedirect.org.uk/museums

Buckie & District Fishing Heritage Centre
The Heritage Cottage, Town Hall Buildings, Cluny Place, Buckie
Banffshire, Scotland AB56 1HB
01542 834702
www.buckieheritage.org

Mersea Island Museum
High Street, West Mersea, Colchester, Essex CO5 8QD
01206 385191
www.merseamuseum.org.uk

Crail Museum and Heritage Centre
62/64 Marketgate, Crail, Anstruther, Fife, Scotland KY10 3TL
01333 450869
www.crailmuseum.org.uk

Cromer Museum
East Cottages, Tucker Street, Cromer, Norfolk NR27 9HB
01263 513543
www.museums.norfolk.gov.uk

Emsworth Museum
10b North Street, Emsworth (near Havant), Hampshire PO10 7DD
01243 378091

Eyemouth Museum
Auld Kirk, Manse Road, Eyemouth, Scottish Borders TD14 5JE, Scotland
01890 750678

National Maritime Museum Cornwall
Discovery Quay, Falmouth, Cornwall TR11 3QY
01326 313388
www.nmmc.co.uk

Filey Museum
8–10 Queen Street, Filey, North Yorkshire YO14 9HB
01723 515013
www.fileybay.com

Fleetwood Museum
Queens Terrace, Fleetwood, Lancashire FY7 6BT
01253 876621
www.lancashire.gov.uk/education/museums/fleetwood

Fraserburgh Heritage Centre
Quarry Road, Fraserburgh, Aberdeenshire, AB43 9DT
01346 514761
www.fraserburghheritage.com

National Maritime Museum
Romney Road, Greenwich, London SE10 9NF
020 8858 4422
www.nmm.ac.uk

National Fishing Heritage Centre
Alexandra Dock, Grimsby, North-East Lincolnshire DN31 1UZ
01472 323345
www.nelincs.gov.uk/leisure/museums/FHC.htm

Museum of Hartlepool
Jackson's Dock Maritime Ave, Hartlepool TS24 0XZ
01429 860077
www.hartlepoolsmaritimeexperience.com

Harwich Maritime Museum
The Low Lighthouse, Harbour Crescent, Harwich, Essex
01255 503429
www.harwich.net/society.htm

Hastings Fishermen's Museum
Rock-a-Nore Road, Hastings, East Sussex TN34 3DW
01424 461446
www.hastingsfish.co.uk/museum.htm

True's Yard Fishing Heritage Centre
North Street, King's Lynn, Norfolk PE30 1QW
01553 770479
www.truesyard.co.uk

Hull Maritime Museum
Queen Victoria Square, Kingston upon Hull, HU1 3DX
1482 613902
www.hullcc.gov.uk/museums

Lancaster Maritime Museum
Custom House, St George's Quay, Lancaster, Lancashire LA1 1RB
01524 382264
www.lancashire.gov.uk/education/museums/lancaster/maritime.asp

Lossiemouth Fisheries and Community Museum
Pitgaveny Quay, Lossiemouth, Moray, Scotland
01343 813772
www.moraymuseumsforum.org.uk

Hull Maritime Museum, situated in the old dock office building. (Author)

Lowestoft and East Suffolk Maritime Heritage Museum
Sparrows Nest Park, Whapload Road, Lowestoft, Suffolk NR32 1XG
01502 561963

Mevagissey Folk Museum
East Wharf, Inner Harbour, Mevagissey, Cornwall
01726 843568
www.cornwall-online.co.uk/restormel/mev-mus.htm

Milford Haven Museum
The Old Custom House, Sybil Way, The Docks, Milford Haven,
Pembrokeshire, SA73 3AF
01646 694496

Montrose Museum
Panmure Place, Montrose, Angus DD10 8HE
01674 673232

Nairn Museum
Viewfield House, Viewfield Drive, Nairn IV12 4EE, Scotland
01667 456791
www.nairnmuseum.co.uk

Newhaven Heritage Museum
The Fishmarket, Newhaven Harbour, Edinburgh, EH8 4IU
0131 551 4165
www.cac.org.uk

Arbuthnot Museum
St. Peter Street, Peterhead, Aberdeenshire, Scotland
01771 622807
www.aberdeenshire.gov.uk/museums/arbuthnot.asp

Peterhead Maritime Heritage
South Road, Lido, Peterhead, Aberdeenshire, Scotland
01779 473000
www.aberdeenshire.gov.uk/museums

Ramsgate Maritime Museum
Clock House, Pier yard, Royal Harbour, Ramsgate, Kent CT11 8LS
01843 570622
www.ekmt.fogonline.co.uk

Marine Life and Fishing Heritage Centre
8–10 Main Street, Seahouses, Northumberland NE68 7RG
01665 721257

Museum Nan Eilean
Francis Street, Stornoway, Isle of Lewis, Western Isles HS1 2NF
01851 709266
www.w-isles.gov.uk/museum.htm

Tolbooth Museum
The Harbour, Stonehaven, Aberdeenshire, Scotland
01771 622906
www.aberdeenshire.gov.uk/museums

Topsham Museum
25 The Strand, Topsham, Exeter, Devon EX3 0AX
01392 873244
www.devonmuseums.net

Watchet Boat Museum
Harbour Road, Watchet, Somerset
01984 633117
www.wbm.org.uk

Whitby Archives and Heritage Centre
The Trinity Centre, Flowergate, Whitby, North Yorkshire YO21 3BA
01947 821364
www.whitbyarchives.org.uk

Whitstable Museum and Gallery
5a Oxford Street, Whitstable, Kent CT5 1DB
01227 276998

Wick Heritage Centre
18–27 Bank Row, Wick, Caithness KW1 5EY, Scotland
01955 605393
www.wickheritage.org

Nottage Maritime Institute
The Quay, Wivenhoe, nr Colchester, Essex CO7 9BX
01206 824142

Appendix Two

FISHING VESSEL PORT LETTERS

A	Aberdeen	CA	Cardigan
AA	Alloa	CE	Coleraine
AB	Aberystwyth	CF	Cardiff
AD	Ardrossan	CH	Chester
AH	Arbroath	CK	Colchester
AR	Ayr	CL	Carlisle
		CN	Campbeltown
B	Belfast	CO	Caernarvon
BA	Ballantrae	CS	Cowes
BCK	Buckie	CY	Castlebay, Barra
BD	Bideford		
BE	Barnstaple	DE	Dundee
BF	Banff	DH	Dartmouth
BH	Blyth	DR	Dover
BK	Berwick-upon-Tweed	DS	Dumfries
BL	Bristol		
BM	Brixham	E	Exeter
BN	Boston		
BO	Borrowstounness	F	Faversham
BR	Bridgewater	FD	Fleetwood
BRD	Broadford	FE	Folkestone
BS	Beaumaris	FH	Falmouth
BU	Burntisland	FR	Fraserburgh
BW	Barrow	FY	Fowey

GE	Goole	NE	Newcastle-upon-Tyne
GH	Grangemouth	NN	Newhaven
GK	Greenock	NT	Newport, Gwent
GN	Granton		
GR	Gloucester	OB	Oban
GW	Glasgow		
GY	Grimsby	P	Portsmouth
		PD	Peterhead
H	Hull	PE	Poole
HH	Harwich	PH	Plymouth
HL	Hartlepool	PN	Preston
		PT	Port Talbot
IE	Irvine	PW	Padstow
IH	Ipswich	PZ	Penzance
INS	Inverness		
		R	Ramsgate
K	Kirkwall	RN	Runcorn
KY	Kirkcaldy	RO	Rothesay
		RR	Rochester
LA	Llanelli	RX	Rye
LH	Leith		
LI	Littlehampton	SA	Swansea
LK	Lerwick	SC	Scilly
LL	Liverpool	SD	Sunderland
LN	King's Lynn	SE	Salcombe
LO	London	SH	Scarborough
LR	Lancaster	SM	Shoreham
LT	Lowestoft	SN	North Shields
LY	Londonderry	SR	Stranraer
		SS	St Ives
M	Milford Haven	SSS	South Shields
ME	Montrose	ST	Stockton
MH	Middlesbrough	SU	Southampton
ML	Methil	SY	Stornoway
MN	Maldon		
MR	Manchester	TH	Teignmouth
		TN	Troon
N	Newry	TO	Truro

TT	Tarbert, Loch Fyne	WI	Wisbech
		WK	Wick
UL	Ullapool	WN	Wigtown
		WO	Workington
WA	Whitehaven	WY	Whitby
WH	Weymouth	YH	Great Yarmouth

Appendix Three

GLOSSARY

Ancillary industries A catch-all term for industries that support the catching effort, such as the supply of necessary goods such as nets, or the processing and marketing of fish.

Barker A person who applied a preservative solution derived from bark to fishing nets.

Bawley Inshore fishing vessel used on the Kent and Essex coasts, chiefly for catching shellfish.

Beatster East Anglian term for those employed making drift nets.

Buss Type of vessel, usually large and square-rigged, used in various offshore fisheries from the fifteenth to early eighteenth centuries.

Black fish Slang term for fish caught over quota and landed illegally.

Bycatch	Fish caught other than that which the vessel is aiming for.
Coble	Inshore craft found on the Yorkshire coast, deep at the bow but flat-bottomed aft for landing stern-first on the beach.
Codbanger	Nineteenth-century term for long-line fishermen, derived from the club used to kill fish before despatch to market.
Coper	A converted fishing smack which plied among the trawling fleets in the North Sea selling cheap tobacco and spirits. Most copers were based in Belgium or the Netherlands.
Cran	A measure of herrings which varied by region from three and a half to four hundredweight.
Dole	Slang term for share of profit in herring fishery.
Cran	A measure of herring, varied according to locality from 3½ to 4 hundredweight.
Crayer	Small, single-masted trading and fishing vessel, a late medieval type which probably died out during the early seventeenth.
Cutter	A type of single-masted sailing rig, also used as a general term for vessels that ferried fish to market from the trawling fleets.

Demersal	Species of fish that live and feed on the sea bed, such as cod, haddock and plaice.
Discarding	The practice of dumping unwanted catches, now illegal under some fishery management regimes.
Dogger, or Drogher	Medieval term for larger fishing craft used for the cod fisheries in the North Sea and off Iceland; also a seventeenth-century term for a two-masted vessel.
Dory	Small, flat-bottomed open boat used for fishing.
Dredge	Small, iron device with a net attached, shaped like a miniature trawl and used for taking shellfish.
Drift-net	Form of gill-net used for catching pelagic species, set along a line at the end of which the vessel drifts with the wind and tide.
Drifter	Vessel deploying drift nets.
Driving/driver	Cornish term for drifting.
Dutch auction	Type of auction by which fish were, and are, frequently sold, at which the auctioneer starts with a high price and reduces it until a bid is made.
Farcosta	Term for a medium-sized medieval fishing craft, used for catching herring in the North Sea.

Fifie	Type of lug-rigged fishing boat used on the east coast of Scotland in the mid-nineteenth century.
Five-man boat	Three-masted, decked lugger found on the Yorkshire coast.
Flatner	Small open boat used in Somerset for estuary and river fishing.
Fleeting	System of trawling whereby vessels fished in fleets and were serviced at regular intervals by cutters, which took the catch to market.
Gill-net	Generic term for nets that trap fish by the gills.
Hand-Line	Long, weighted line with one or more baited hooks attached, operated by hand for catching cod.
Hoggie/Hog boat	Type of two-masted inshore fishing vessel used on the Sussex coast.
Hooker/hooking	General term for inshore line-fishing, and the boats used for it.
Joskins	Old term used in East Anglia for seasonal workers in the herring fishery, usually farmhands.
Jowder/Jowster	Cornish term for an itinerant fish seller.
Last	A measure of herring, equating to around two tons.

Long-line	Method of fishing whereby baited hooks are attached to a line, sometimes several miles long, that is set on the sea bed.
Lugger	Technical term for a sailing vessel rig, usually used on small craft. A wide variety of lug-rigged vessels were used around Britain in pelagic and inshore fisheries.
Mule	Brixham term for a smaller sailing trawler, as distinct from larger ones known locally as 'sloops'.
Mumble Bee	Small, single-masted inshore sailing trawler, so called because such boats from Tenby and sometimes Brixham trawled in Mumbles Bay.
Murage	Special tax or toll levied by royal licence for the maintenance of town fortifications; sometimes demanded of visiting fishing vessels.
Nickey/Nobby	Two types of fast lugger used for fishing from the Isle of Man.
Offal	Nineteenth-century term for cheaper varieties of whitefish such as cod and haddock, as distinct from 'prime' species.
Overfishing	A situation where a fish stock is being fished at a faster rate than it is able to reproduce.

Pair-trawling	Trawling by two vessels, each handling one warp of a large trawl.
Parish apprentice	An apprentice indentured by the parish authorities which administered the Poor Law. Parish, or pauper, apprentices usually came from workhouses and similar institutions.
Pelagic	Species of fish that shoal near to the surface of the sea, such as herring, pilchard and mackerel.
Poundage	Means of payment common in trawl fisheries: a share of the proceeds of the voyage over and above the basic wage.
Prime	Valuable species of whitefish, especially soles and halibut, contrasted with 'offal'.
Quintal	An ancient measure, usually used for salted or dried cod or stockfish, equating to about 112 lb.
Quota	Amount of fish allowed to each vessel under various fishery management regimes, including the Common Fisheries Policy.
Scaffie	Type of lug-rigged fishing boat used in north and east Scotland in the mid-nineteenth century.
Seine	Term covering various types of net used to enclose shoals of fish, operated either from the beach or from a vessel.

Ship's husband	A shore worker, generally employed by a larger firm, responsible for ensuring a boat was properly serviced in port, usually responsible for arranging supplies and recruiting crews.
Share/shares system	Payment by a proportion of the proceeds of a voyage, usually varying according to an individual's position in the crew.
Shooting	General term for the casting of nets or lines.
Sloop	A single-masted sailing vessel rig, also used at Brixham as a colloquial term for the larger class of sailing trawler
Smack	Sail-driven fishing vessel, usually referring to a wooden cutter- or ketch-rigged trawler or dredger. Sometimes used as a generic term for a small fishing, or sometimes coastal trading, vessel.
Stocker/stockerbait	Trawling term for small and unmarketable fish sold other than through the main fish market, usually by the crew for their own profit.
Stow-net/stowboat	A method of fishing for sprats used in Essex, whereby a stocking-shaped net was rigged under an anchored vessel.
Target species	The main species of fish targeted by a fishing voyage, as distinct from bycatch.

Trawl

Conical net towed behind a fishing vessel. The mouth of the net is held open either by a beam (beam trawl) or by otter boards, or 'doors', attached to either side (otter trawl). Trawls were originally used on the sea bed only, but more recently mid-water trawls have been developed.

Trawler

Vessel fishing with a trawl.

Well

A section of the hull of a boat sealed off with watertight bulkheads and the outer hull pierced to allow seawater to circulate, for the purpose of keeping fish alive inside.

Zulu

Scottish fishing boat type combining the characteristics of the fifie and scaffie, introduced around 1880.

INDEX